HANDBOOK OF PRACTICAL POLITICS

We will never bring disgrace to this our city, by any act of dishonesty or cowardice, nor ever desert our comrades; we will fight for the ideals and sacred things of the city, both alone and with many; we will revere and obey the city laws, and do our best to incite a like respect and reverence in others; we will strive unceasingly to quicken the public's sense of civic duty; that thus in all these ways, we may transmit this city, greater, better, and more beautiful than it was transmitted to us.

The Athenian Oath of Citizenship

Handbook of
PRACTICAL
POLITICS

THIRD
EDITION

PAUL P. VAN RIPER

*Graduate School of Business and Public
Administration, Cornell University*

HARPER & ROW, PUBLISHERS
NEW YORK, EVANSTON, AND LONDON

To
Dorothy and Scott

Acknowledgments

Acknowledgment is gratefully made to the following agents, authors, and publishers who have granted permission to reprint excerpts from copyrighted publications.

Gus Tyler, "American Politics: How They Work and How You Can Work in Them," in *Guide to Politics—1954*, The Dial Press, New York, 1954, pp. 126 and 176–178; and Gus Tyler, "Getting into Politics," in *Voting Guide—1956*, Americans for Democratic Action, Washington, D.C., 1956, p. 128. Elmo Roper and Julian L. Woodward, "Political Activity of American Citizens," *American Political Science Review*, December, 1950, Charts IV and V, pp. 877 and 878. Leone Baxter, "Public Relations' Precocious Baby," *The Public Relations Journal*, copyright, January, 1950, p. 18. Robert E. Merriam and Rachel M. Goetz, *Going into Politics*, Harper & Row, Publishers, Incorporated, New York, 1957, pp. 39–40 and 203–204. Raymond Moley, *The Political Responsibility of Businessmen*, pp. 35–36 of the 1958 edition and pp. 32–33 of the 1959–1960 edition. *Republican Campaign Manual*, published by the Republican National Committee, Washington, D.C., 1950, pp. 56–59, 67–70, 75–77, and 82–84. Daniel J. Riesner, *Practical Politics*, New York, 1950, pp. 40–41 (former President, National Republican Club; former Secretary, New York Republican County Committee; senior member law firm of Riesner, Jawitz and Holland). The John Day Company for the selections from *How to Go into Politics* by Hugh D. Scott, Jr., pp. 15–16, 17, and 18–20, copyright © 1949 by Hugh D. Scott, Jr., by permission of The John Day Company, Inc., publisher.

Contents

Preface

This book is intended for the individual concerned about his community or government, the student, the civic or political volunteer, the political amateur, the civic-minded group, and the political club and club member. It is also designed as a guide to those who aspire to professional status in the world of democratic political action, and as a checklist and reminder for those to whom politics is a vocation.

The aim here is to bring out and treat systematically many of the problems of organizing for effective citizen action—partisan or nonpartisan—at the grass roots level. This is neither a book in political theory and issues nor a study of national politics and parties. Rather, it is planned to attack the numerous and often detailed problems of practical politics at their source, the bottom segments of the political pyramid.

About the organization of this book, two things need to be said. First, it is designed to let the experts in political action speak for themselves as much as possible through extensive excerpts from the best of their professional literature, most of which is not available to the average citizen. Second, the first three chapters cover primarily the reasons and opportunities for political action, so that if you are already convinced of the importance of such action, or perhaps even started in a small civic or political way, you may wish to move directly to Chapter 4.

That is, the early chapters are mainly concerned with the various possibilities of political action and the personal decisions often required of those entering the political arena. But the bulk of the book, beginning with Chapter 4, "How to

Get Started," relates to the actual workings of practical politics. This recognizes that most of the difficulties facing the person interested in effective political action stem from a lack of knowledge about "how to do it."

This edition has also been specially designed to take into account a number of trends and tendencies that have become clearly discernible since the publication of the first edition in 1952. The most important of these is the increasingly fluid nature of American politics, characterized by less interest in patronage, a greater concern with issues, and an advancing amount of independent voting, which has underscored the need for carefully planned civic and political organization at every level for all causes. Less and less can be left to chance, habit, or tradition. In addition, our rapidly expanding population means that ever greater numbers of people must be appealed to. This has meant a growing use of all forms of public relations media, especially television, backed, in turn, by research on an unprecedented scale. The spectacular development of mass organizational and manipulative techniques derived from market research, merchandising, and the social sciences has rapidly brought to the fore the professional public relations agencies with their "Madison Avenue" approach. Some firms now specialize almost exclusively in political action work.

However, along with increasing professionalism at the center of political organization has come a new emphasis on the role of the volunteer. There has been something of a renaissance in political activity, throughout the country, on the part of women, young people, and, most recently, businessmen. Moreover, as additional numbers of people have to be reached through further expensive means of communication, the postwar emphasis on the utilization of rising numbers of volunteers and the development of more broadly based political financing has been steadily reinforced. The materials which follow have been selected to reflect these trends.

Finally, it is important to stress that this book is concerned only with the *why* and *how* of political action; *what* and *whom* the individual votes for are his own business, as far as this book is concerned. There is no attempt here to take sides on parties, candidates, or issues. But it is everybody's business that we all understand what is involved in finding our way around the world of civic and political action.

PAUL P. VAN RIPER

Chapter 1

The
Chance of
Success

Life and politics in our democracy are the results of an accumulation of decisions made by millions of citizens from every corner of the country in every walk of life. Only in a democracy do individual citizens have an opportunity to participate in deciding the really important issues facing them. Indeed, this is the very essence of democracy.

Nevertheless, practically speaking, how much of an opportunity is there in the United States to do more than just vote? It is all well and good to advocate civic and political action, but what about the chances for the individual citizen to break into the political game?

In assessing the possibility of grass roots political action, it is important to consider

1. *the basic characteristics of "the system"* and
2. *its general organization structure.*

1

1. THE AMERICAN POLITICAL SYSTEM

Political parties in the United States are highly decentralized affairs, reflecting a multiplicity of interests held together less by theory and principle than by compromise and practicle give and take on matters of mutual concern at the time. Our Constitution provides for a federal system of government in which certain important kinds of authority are specifically left to the individual states rather than the national government. To be sure, Congress has the power to regulate many things concerning elections for federal offices such as those of the President, Vice-President, congressmen, and senators. In all elections the Constitution has for a long time forbade voting discrimination on the grounds of race, religion, previous condition of servitude, and sex; and current civil rights legislation has put teeth into these provisions. Moreover, the recent Twenty-fourth Amendment provides that you cannot be charged money—in the form of a poll tax—for the right to vote for candidates for national offices, and a March, 1966 decision of the Supreme Court has outlawed the poll tax in state and local elections.

Nevertheless, the states, by a mixture of law and custom, have most of the say-so about the setting up of our election system, nomination procedures, and the legal rules which political organizations must follow. And, despite recent federal legislation, the states still have considerable authority concerning who shall vote and under what circumstances. That is, in general outline and in nearly all details *the political process in the United States is a state process*, governed by state law, with each state somewhat different from the others. This fact, plus the absence of any other controls which can be exercised by a national party chairman or committee over the state and local segments of a party, means that *any central control of American political parties is quite limited*.

What does this decentralization suggest for the individual who wants to try his hand at political action? Under such a system it is easy for the single individual, the political outsider, the newcomer, to break into the political game. You do not have to crack a tightly knit national organization in order to throw your political weight around, as you have to do in England, Germany, Italy, and most of the rest of the world where political organization is heavily centralized.

The fact that in most states we also have the *primary system* of nominations makes this "breaking-in" process even easier. For in a primary, an individual does not have to get the approval of even the local party leaders in order to take a shot at, for instance, the Republican nomination for county sheriff or the Democratic nomination for state senator.

Our politics has its roots in state and local government rather than in the national government. The centers of political power are in the states and their subunits. This is why Senator Frank J. Lausche of Ohio and Senator Edward M. Kennedy of Massachusetts can sport the same political tag, and why Senator Jacob K. Javits of New York and former Senator Barry Goldwater of Arizona can both use the Republican label. This is why Senator Wayne Morse of Oregon could change from Republican to Democrat so easily, and Senator Strom Thurmond of South Carolina from Democrat to Republican, and why the late Mayor Fiorello LaGuardia was able to run under a grand total of nine different party labels—and under as many as four at one time.

Each of these men has been supreme in his own bailiwick. There has been nothing that anybody could do about it except the voters in that bailiwick.

Now this does not mean that you can ignore the party organization completely and get anywhere either. It merely means that, if you play your cards right, you have a good chance of breaking into that organization or of influencing it in the direction you would like to see it take.

It is always simpler, of course, if you can operate through an existing organization. This saves you the trouble of building up another and competing organization. It means that you will have other people with you who have experience in all the things this book is about. And, as the party organization which already exists is better organized and more permanently organized than anything it normally competes against, you have to be pretty well organized yourself in order successfully to buck it.

But the important thing to remember is—that it is possible to buck it or, better yet, to capture it.

Let us take a brief look, then, at some of the organizational details of this "system" and see more precisely what we must either deal with or make terms with or fight with.

2. PARTY ORGANIZATION STRUCTURE

Fortunately for ease in understanding American politics, in spite of the fact that our party system is extremely decentralized, we have developed certain basic similarities in party organization throughout the country. Even though each state or local area may differ from every other area in the details of its political mechanism, there are some general characteristics of the American party system which are pretty much uniform wherever you run up against them.

These general characteristics are briefly and well described in the following paragraphs. Substitute "Democratic" or "Liberal" or any other party label in place of "Republican" and you still have the basic system. This is taken from a pamphlet called *Forward & Right—a Handbook for Women Leaders of the Republican Party Organization*, published a few years ago by the Women's Division of the Republican National Committee.

What's in a Vote?

The Republican party organization begins with the people. The smallest political subdivision is called a "precinct," "ward," or "election district," but for purposes of this handbook the term "precinct" will be used.

The Republican voters start the machinery in the precinct caucus. From there is built a system of party conventions, committees, and party primary elections. The conventions (county, state, and national) govern the party. They establish a line of policy and delegate powers to committees to carry out the adopted policies. The members of the party committees and their officers are elected, and their duties are outlined by state law, or in some cases by party rules. The fact that this organization is set up by law, or by party rules written by representatives of all Republicans, gives its members and leaders specific powers and responsibilities to lead all party activities. This organization is called the "official organization," the "regular organization," or the "statutory organization."

The duties and powers of the Republican precinct caucus vary in different states. They are open to all voters who legally qualify as Republican party members. In some states a voter must be registered as a Republican. In states which do not have partisan registration, he may be required to declare that he considers himself a Republican and adheres to the broad policies of the Republican party. These bona fide Republican members in the precinct meet and *nominate* a precinct committeeman and committeewoman. These committee members may be elected by the same caucus, or they may be elected in a primary election.

The *primary election* is an election in which the party selects members for certain party committees, delegates to party conventions, and candidates for public office.

The next step above the precinct committee in the party organization is the *county central committee*. (Some communities, especially large ones, have a "city committee.") There are several methods of choosing its members and the method used in each state is established by state law or party rule. There may be a county convention, composed of delegates selected by the precinct caucuses, or it may be composed of all the precinct committee members; candidates for membership in the county committee may be required formally to file papers and be elected in the primary; or a variation of these methods may be prescribed. The county central committeemen and women elect a chairman who is the *leader of the party in the county.* Most counties also elect a woman vice-chairman, who directs women's activities under the leadership of the chairman.

Many states have *congressional committees,* elected usually at congressional district conventions. In most instances these are advisory in character. They advise with the congressional candidate, keep track of the progress of the ·campaign, and make sure that adequate publicity is given the candidate; that the candidate has the chance to meet the leaders in every community in his district; and that the county and local committees are working diligently for the candidate's success.

Next above the county central is the *state central committee.* Its members are usually chosen by the county conventions or in the primary election. The state committee elects a chairman, although in some states he is appointed by the candidate for governor. Nearly all states have a woman state vice-chairman who, working in close cooperation with the chairman, heads the state's women's division and directs women's work in the state.

Nationally, the party organization is headed by the *Republican National Committee.* It is composed of one man and one woman member from each state and territory. These members may be nominated by (1) state convention; (2) state committee; (3) primary election; (4) by the state's delegates to the national convention. These nominees are *elected* by the Republican National Convention which is held every four years. When a vacancy on the committee occurs, the state committee *nominates* a successor, and the Republican National Committee formally *elects* the nominee at its next meeting.

The Republican National Committee is the governing body of the party at the national level between national conventions. It elects its chairman who is the active head of the party. It calls the national convention and makes all arrangements for holding it. The assistant chairman of the Republican National Committee must be a woman and she is director of its women's division. She may be elected by the committee, although the committee traditionally gives the chairman power of appointment. By rule of the Republican National Convention, all subcommittees of the national committee must be composed of an equal number of men and women.

The *Republican National Convention* is made up of delegates from all states and territories. These delegates may be elected by a state-wide primary, state convention, or the state committee. Their principal duties are (1) to nominate the party's candidates for President and Vice-President of the United States; (2) to adopt a party platform; and (3) to elect the Republican National Committee, and adopt rules to govern it.

The purpose of this structure of committees and conventions is to provide the means whereby the rank and file of Republicans may, through their *chosen representatives or delegates, nominate the best and strongest candidates for public office, and then elect them.*

As you can see, this is an open organizational arrangement run from the bottom up rather than from the top down.

3. CONCLUSION

To sum up—our political "system" in the United States is a decentralized one, composed of several layers of cooperative committees. It is this fluid nature of our political organization which gives it that air of mystery to the uninitiated.

But the very fact that it is decentralized, that it does vary somewhat from state to state and locality to locality, and that it never seems to stand still are the guarantees that the individual has a chance when it comes to politics. Many European political party systems are unified, relatively simple to understand, and almost impossible for the amateur or the outsider to break into. Our party system may seem complex at first glance, but it is one in which it is extremely difficult for the leaders at the top to avoid paying attention to those at the bottom.

In this country, the individual has a chance in politics if he wants to take it. And it is our decentralized "system" which, above all, makes this possible.

Chapter 2

Partisan
or
Independent?

The preceding chapter has stressed the importance of political parties and of working within them. However, in recent years there has been a trend in American politics toward so-called "independent" voting and action.

Here we will consider the relative merits of two kinds of political action associated with the concept of "independence," as opposed to the merits of working within the established parties. Expressed in terms of alternatives, we will consider the approaches of

1. *the "independent" versus the "regular"* and
2. *the nonpartisan versus the partisan.*

Your decision with respect to these alternatives will have a good deal to do both with the direction any political action on your part is likely to take and with the setting in which you will find yourself.

1. THE "INDEPENDENT" v. THE "REGULAR"

The hallmarks of *the independent* are the "split ticket" and "scratching," terms used to describe an individual's casting his ballot partly for the nominees of one party and partly for those of another. This is in opposition to "voting a straight ticket," the sign of *the regular*, a person who almost always votes only for the candidates of his own political party. The independent usually claims either no party allegiance or at most a temporary and fluctuating one.

Actually there are degrees of independence and regularity. Some voters frequently split their ticket but, from election to election, alternate back and forth between parties; others vote only occasionally for a candidate of a party other than their own. The independent rejects constant affiliation with one party, but he does not reject voting itself. Though the party regular may court the vote of the independent, he is apt to look upon the independent as a "free-rider," much in the same way an active union member may think of the non-union worker. There are a good many arguments both ways.

One of the clearest discussions of the problem of independence versus party regularity is contained in the pamphlet, *Is Politics Your Job?* published a few years ago by the League of Women Voters. The discussion is in dialogue form, with the *independent* stating,

> I am a mugwump—one of those awful birds with his mug on one side of the political fence and his wump on the other.
>
> I seldom vote a straight ticket, I gather bits and shreds of information like mad before each election, read all the news items, the polls, the prognosticators. I go to candidates' meetings, listen to radio speeches, read everybody's campaign fliers as if my life depended on it. . . . My eyes are focused on the issues, understanding them and deciding how I stand on them. After that I judge the men and the parties.

The *regular* replies,

> Most Americans, but particularly independent voters,
> are inclined to place entirely too much emphasis on candi-
> dates themselves and their personalities and not enough
> emphasis on what they stand for. . . . The record shows
> that the most important influence on a man's voting
> behavior is the party to which he belongs.

> • • • • • •

> Independent voters, because they have no connection
> with a party, do not realize the decisive influence that a
> man's party has on his voting behavior. Independent
> voters are not only likely to misjudge candidates, but they
> fail to do their share prior to voting. Mugwumps refuse
> all responsibility for the selection of candidates. They
> only arrive on the scene at election time. . . . If every-
> body were a mugwump, we wouldn't have any parties
> or any candidates.

The editor then summarizes the argument, noting that "each
outlook has a marked effect on voting percentages and election results."

> The independent voter may be an erratic voter, going
> to the polls only when the election is a "hot" one or when
> he feels strongly disposed about a single candidate or
> issue. On the other hand, he may as easily be a conscien-
> tious, informed citizen (not unlike the mugwump) who
> simply finds affiliation with a political party personally
> unpalatable. There could be many reasons for his reluc-
> tance to join a party. . . . In any case, the independent
> voter is a power to be reckoned with.
> Both major parties make a practice of courting him. . . .
> Party platforms and campaign promises are built on
> hopes of tempting the independent and his fellow irreg-
> ulars into the party camp. . . .
> Is this to imply that all the advantages are on the side
> of the independent? We need only look back on the
> comment of the loyal party worker to remember that
> this is not necessarily so. The independent in a real sense
> is an outsider when it comes to politics. By dint of his

aloofness from the parties, he is excluded from helping hammer out party decisions. Caucuses, informal party discussions, conventions and even primary elections are beyond his influence, for it is in these functions of the party that candidates and platforms are first brought to the fore. The independent, for all practical purposes, must be content to make a secondary choice between alternatives which party members place before him. He is seldom really "in" on grass-roots political activities.

Both the party regular and the independent, then, have arguments to muster in support of their respective political convictions. In the end, it is up to you as an individual citizen to weigh the pros and cons of voting the party or the nonparty way.

The political parties, of course, take a much more positive stand against independence. In their leaflet, *Why Be Interested in Politics*, the Young Democratic Clubs of America argue:

It follows that the man who keeps out of politics, who sanctimoniously takes pride in his "independence" is in fact forfeiting a sizable amount of his independence by being deprived of the privilege of helping determine candidates and issues in conventions and primaries. His final choices are limited by a process in which he has no part. The most independent individual is the person of independent *judgment* who takes part in the entire political process which includes full participation in the party of his choice.

In the recent New Jersey *Republican Handbook* party regulars are advised to take this approach with independents:

If they say: "I'm an independent . . . I do my own thinking. . . . "
You say: "Fine . . . but did you ever stop to think of how candidates get their names on the ballot? They are put on by partisan voters. Independents, who want to think for themselves, are in the position of second-guessing on Party choices, and wind up accepting and rejecting someone else's candidate. Full political expression

comes only when a voter participates actively in one of the two parties in a constructive manner."

In reality, much so-called independent voting represents the occasional splitting of tickets, on behalf of only one or two candidates, by voters more or less committed to, rather than fully independent of, the major political parties. The best arguments against this less virulent form of independence are similar to those below against nonpartisanship.

2. THE NONPARTISAN v. THE PARTISAN

The term "nonpartisan" is used in so many ways that it is often confusing. But to be most nearly correct, nonpartisanship explicitly recognizes the need for some sort of organized political action. The nonpartisan objects only to working under the traditional party labels.

In its excellent and forthright booklet, *The Citizen Association: How to Organize and Run It*, the National Municipal League says:

> How deep into political action you go will depend partly on the needs of the community and partly on the attitude of your supporters. Don't be overly cautious. There is nothing to be gained by watering down a program to make it palatable to the most timid citizens.
>
> Political action should not be feared or avoided. Politics is simply the science or art of government. A citizen association that eschews politics places itself in the unhappy position of the young lady whose mother admonished her to hang her clothes on the hickory limb but not to go near the water.

It is generally agreed that the case for nonpartisan civic and political action is strongest at the community level, where those engaged in such work know each other and where the issues cut across party lines. If carried beyond the strictly local level, nonpartisanship begins to lose much of its meaning and usefulness. One of the major functions of political parties is to assist us in defining issues and electing representatives in situations where we may not know personally many of the persons involved or where issues are such as to require statewide or nationwide discussion in order to resolve them. The national parties are also equipped to handle many issues at one time, while the typical civic group is likely to pinpoint its effort at a single problem, such as a new charter, better schools, or juvenile delinquency.

However, nonpartisan civic associations and political parties are by no means mutually exclusive. The former may often serve as a gadfly and spur to get needed political action in a community where there has been none. And the latter may be essential if the solution to a community problem lies higher up—in the county government, the state legislature, or the national capital.

Coming back again to the National Municipal League's manual for citizen associations:

> In many cities, voters who bear different labels in national elections work shoulder to shoulder for sound, nonpartisan local government. They recognize that there is no Democratic way to put out a fire and no Republican technique for digging a sewer. These citizens have developed a deep sense of pride in their status as amateur politicians devoted to the public welfare. And they have earned a double reward: the satisfaction of achievement and the respect of their neighbors.

The final case for forthright partisan action completely within the traditional parties has been most bluntly and cogently stated by Professor E. E. Schattschneider of Wesleyan University, a former president of the American Political Science Association, in his outspoken booklet, *The Struggle for Party Government.*

> Since we start with the assumption that the political base for an effective government must be created by a mobilization of the nation, it follows that we are looking

for the kind of political organization which can reach the whole country. . . . the only kind of organization that can translate into fact the idea of majority rule is the political party. The parties are unique in this respect. They create and mobilize majorities; they define the alternatives and enable the nation to make decision; they submit themselves to the will of the nation in elections. By every democratic standard the parties are the proper means for producing a political solution of the government crisis.

• • • • • •

The major party is the only political organization in American life which is in a position to make a claim, upon any reasonable grounds whatsoever, that it can measure up to the requirements of modern public policy. The party alone pretends to be interested in a general control of the government; only the party possesses the kind of power required to make the government work; it alone might reasonably be held responsible for the general state of public policy. Of all the varieties of political organization, it alone gets a mandate from the people to govern the country. If we believe in majority rule, we are bound to believe also in the only practicable means by which majority rule can be implemented. *Party government is therefore as right as democracy itself.* It follows that party organization and party techniques for getting control of the government, and the measures necessary to the creation of an effective party system, are admirable, for we cannot believe that party government is a good thing without also believing in the means appropriate to the end.

3. CONCLUSION

For various reasons—you may, for example, be a civil servant who is forbidden by law from being in partisan politics —you may not find it possible to be active in the party of your choice. Or your abilities and interests may lie elsewhere. After all, it is crucial that someone fight to keep polio under control and that others lend their talents to the community chest, the chamber of commerce, labor unions, veterans organizations, and the churches.

But, ultimately, the maintenance of a strong democracy is dependent upon a strong system of political parties. This, in turn, must be based on widespread citizen concern with and participation in partisan party affairs.

Chapter 3

The Personal Challenge

Even if you accept the need for political action, there immediately arises the problem of what personal involvement may mean. That is: What do I stand to gain? What can I lose?

Let us therefore consider here

1. the major *personal hazards* you may encounter in politics, and
2. the possible *benefits and rewards*.

1. DIFFICULTIES AND DILEMMAS

Admittedly, politics has its special problems. These can be summed up under three charges: politics is synonymous with (1) money, (2) dirt, and (3) moral corruption. Let us consider these in order.

Can I Afford It Financially?

The problem is not great if you plan to work at politics mainly on a part-time basis in your home community. In this situation the out-of-pocket costs will be minimal, probably no more than you might spend on any other avocation. Your time, your services and those of your family, and your car will be your main contributions and they may be all you need. Friends are often available to assist on a Dutch treat basis.

It is when you consider entering the full-fledged professional ranks that the financial problem may become really perplexing. While the professional is not our main object of concern here, perhaps it is just as well to view political life occasionally in its fullest perspective. Politics as a career, or even partial career, brings to bear long-run financial considerations. About these, Stimson Bullitt, a young Seattle lawyer and businessman with considerable political experience in the Democratic party at state and local levels, has made some pertinent observations in his book, *To Be a Politician* (1959). This is one of the most perceptive works available on the personal problems deriving from fulltime political life.

> In politics the rate of pay is modest, although not as low as one might think from the complaints of some. Expense is high and much is not tax deductible. Because, unlike happiness, money-making can best be achieved by direct approach, politics is no place for anyone who wants to make big money, or, unless he has it already, to live on a scale of comfort which requires it. The main loss of income caused by politics is not the drop, if any, in the actual net income on entering public office. It is rather that following a period of political activity the long-run level of private income tends to be below what it would have been if the person had stayed where he was and polished the handle of the big front door. Although having done time in politics is likely to reduce a person's total lifetime income, this loss, because evenly spread and deferred to future years, is a weaker deterrent than the conditions, say, of becoming a physician, where the austerity comes at the start.

For the long haul, there is almost unanimous agreement that a politician must have an alternative source of income. This is necessary not only to support himself and his family should he fail in an election, but for another important reason to which Bullitt has called attention.

> The most important reason for starting as a part-time apprentice is that one may at the same time learn politics and another trade. The risk is slight that one will stay an amateur so long that he becomes a dabbler. The choice does not matter much, but a private calling is essential to the politician who is brave and wishes to be free. Like Cincinnatus, he should have a plow standing ready for him in a field at home. This goes for everyone, despite the independence of his means. A strong-willed politician's flesh is too weak not to be chilled by the prospect of a long drop. Without a happy alternative, an acrobat's net, he cannot afford the independent judgment which he must have to do his duty.

If you are seeking a nomination or contesting for one in a primary, you and your personal backers must raise your own funds. The party normally will not support you in any way until you are in fact the party's nominee. Even if you win the nomination, considerable financial responsibility may fall upon you. This can be a tremendous burden, especially if you are running "against the tide" in your area.

In their book, *How to Get Into Politics* (1946), Oliver Carlson and Aldrich Blake say, with a good deal of truth, the campaign funds are made up of (1) coppers from the general public, (2) nickels from the personal friends of the candidate, (3) silver from persons who want revenge on your rival, and (4) gold from those who want something from you if you win.

But how does this work out in practice? For general procedure see Chapter 7. An illuminating case history is provided, however, by Robert E. Merriam, a former Chicago alderman who in 1955 was asked to become the Republican candidate for mayor in predominately Democratic Chicago.

Before agreeing to run, Merriam inquired into the probable costs of a campaign and was informed that $500,000 would be required. Not far from that sum was raised. The full story is given in his (and Rachel M. Goetz's) book, *Going Into Politics* (1957). Especially relevant here are Merriam's comments on "expectations" in return for "investment."

> How is such a sum of money raised, and what do the contributors expect from their investment? Actually, in this campaign over three thousand individual contributors participated, from a low of ten cents provided by an elementary school girl to a contribution of well in excess of $10,000. All the traditional means of raising money were employed: direct mail solicitation, personal calls, and a fundraising dinner which netted over $80,000. . . .
>
> Some contributors of substantial sums obviously gave to both candidates to insure, so they hoped, fair treatment of their interests no matter who was elected. Generally these were interests having, at some point, direct contact with the city. Some contributors hoped to have a friend in court in time of need, and my position was always that "if you have legitimate business with the city, I'll never penalize you for having helped me; but don't count on any special assistance." Because of my fight on organized crime, no direct approaches were made by the syndicate (which has been a potent influence in the Chicago area). But one man representing himself as part of a racket which was being invaded by the syndicate let it be known through an intermediary that he was willing to raise $50,000 from his associates, not on the guarantee of protection from the law but on the understanding that the syndicate be "taken off their back." This sum was not accepted.
>
> Despite the most rigid of economy steps, which prevented our doing many things we had hoped to do, and despite the multifold fundraising activities, the week before election found us with no money for election day purposes. My campaign manager, the Republican county chairman, and I met in serious conference to determine how to find the money to finish the campaign. At the

eleventh hour a great citizen offered to borrow, on his signature, $67,000 with which to meet these needs. Not many people are willing, unselfishly, wanting nothing whatever for themselves, to take that kind of risk! This loan and $33,000 of unpaid bills were a legacy from the campaign. A postelection banquet (eight hundred people at $50 per plate feted the defeated candidate) helped to defray part of that cost. I was overwhelmed by the turn-out. As the governor himself said at the banquet, "There are times when I haven't been able to get anyone to buy me a hamburger when I lost."

Isn't Politics Dirty?

Dr. Lee C. McDonald's reply to Pomona College students in his *Student's Guide to Practical Politics* may answer this question.

> *Well, is politics a dirty business?* Yes and no. If you mean by "dirty" that politicians are mostly a bunch of crooks for whom graft is a profitable sideline or that crucial elections are often won by stuffing the ballot box, then the answer is no. As a group, politicians are probably as honest in their dealings with other people as bottle-cap manufacturers, deep-sea divers, or college professors. Besides, bribery is not in good taste these days. Among political leaders and workers you will find realists and idealists, egoists and altruists, heathens and Christians, bright-boys and knuckleheads. If anything, they will be a little more human than usual.
>
> . . . . . .
>
> On the other hand, if you mean by dirty: compromise of ideals, organized selfish interests fighting each other, ambitious men who over-simplify the truth in order to win favor, then the answer is yes. ". . . politics ain't bean bag," as Mr. Dooley well observed; but then neither is life. The above phenomena can be observed in realms other than political—a school, a business, a labor union, a fraternity, a church. Yet, as two young political scientists have pointed out, "We cannot . . . take the position that just because the world is not foolproof against ethical seasickness, we'll refuse to sail at all."

Part of the problem lies in the fact that we apply a double standard of conduct in judging public and private affairs. In business, for example, it is normally considered quite proper to use to your own advantage any information which comes your way, and no one would criticize you for so doing. But in public life, the Secretary of the Treasury, for example, had better not speculate in government bonds. Moreover, if you are in politics of any sort your life is apt to be more of an open book than is the case in other occupations.

Finally, the rest of the problem derives from the fact that politics represents the center of power. Whoever controls the government controls much of our lives. The stakes are high. The temptation to play rough is accordingly great, and this brings us to the next question.

What About My Convictions?

Dr. McDonald hinted at this when he mentioned the word "compromise." That is: What about your convictions? Must you inevitably sacrifice them in political life?

The first part of any answer to this question has been bluntly delivered by Senator Edmund S. Muskie of Maine: "Do convictions and politics mix? Yes, if the politician has convictions. There is, of course, no problem at all if you have no basic principles to which you hold."

But, if you feel rather deeply about certain things are you likely to have to compromise your principles? If you have rather narrow principles and hold to them rigidly, the answer is often yes. The late T. V. Smith, a former Democratic congressman from Illinois as well as a distinguished professor of political science, believed: "A man is not a good man who will compromise the core of himself—that is, the final principles by which he lives. But a man is not a good citizen who does not meet other citizens half way."

One of the basic functions of a politician at any level is to represent others. A political worker is expected to carry out his constituents' principles as much as he does his own. This is the essence of representative government. But reconciling differing sets of guidelines and beliefs is no easy matter.

Political action is strewn with this kind of moral dilemma. The advice offered by Lowell Mellett, a veteran newspaper reporter and former administrative assistant to President Franklin D. Roosevelt, is perhaps the best available. In his *Handbook of Politics* (1946), published shortly after World War II, he strongly recommends that "if you are not tolerant enough to work with people you don't like, there is not much use" in your considering going into any aspect of politics or, for that matter, almost any kind of civic action involving the bringing together of people with diverse views and interests.

> If you would rather be right than President, that is easy, but somebody has to be President (and congressman), and what are you going to do about that?
>
> . . . . . .
>
> Pick an organization that is out for blood, even if you don't agree with some of its ideas. . . . Not everybody who is fighting to beat the present incumbent is doing it for reasons with which you would agree.
>
> . . . . . .
>
> But what about your principles? The useful tactical principle is that of never voting for a bad man for re-election, and always supporting the man who can defeat him. Since this is useful to your country, it becomes your political duty, and it is probably a lot more moral than merely expressing your own feelings without accomplishing anything.
>
> . . . . . .
>
> Keep your mind on the purpose that will serve the public interest, not on your own personal ego, or the ego of your pet candidate. When a champion has been chosen to lead your army, drop your family arguments and get behind your leader. You can be sure the opposition forces will forget their personal feelings and face the real issue of victory or defeat. Their selfishness is intelligent; if yours is stupid you will lose and will deserve to.

This kind of hard, cold advice concerning how to be effective in politics is difficult for many people to understand, let alone take. In politics, public rather than private personal interests must govern.

If you can work with others and to some extent subordinate self to organization and the practical requirements of winning an election, then you may have a real opportunity to make some impression on public life in your community or elsewhere. For, basically, *politics is the art of the possible.*

The former Democratic Senator from Connecticut and Assistant Secretary of State, William Benton analyzes the problem in his discussion of "The Big Dilemma: Conscience or Votes" in the April 26, 1959, issue of *The New York Times Magazine.*

> In my judgment it is often impossible for a legislator clearly to separate considerations of prudence from moral principles. Indeed, he must frequently fall back on prudence if he is to advance his moral principles. . . .
>
> Abraham Lincoln never doubted that slavery was wrong. Yet in December, 1860, a month after his election as President, he offered to guarantee to the Southern states, in perpetuity, their right to a slave system, providing they agreed there should be no extension of slavery in the territories. Lincoln hoped that this offer might avert civil war; and undoubtedly he hoped also that the slave system would in time dissolve and disappear.

2. THE POSITIVE SIDE

This leads to the possible benefits and rewards for the participant in politics and civic action.

If you happen to be a lawyer, insurance salesman, or retailer, you may profit financially from engaging in politics. There is much truth in a remark attributed to Marvin Rosenberry, a former chief justice of the Wisconsin supreme court. In their book, *Plunging Into Politics* (1964), Marshall Loeb and William Safire report Rosenberry as once joking "that the best counsel he could offer to a young lawyer would be for him to run for prosecuting attorney, but be sure not to win. The election publicity—'ethical advertising'—would call attention to his law practice."

More important, however, if you believe in some basic principles and have some ability, the world of politics provides one of the greatest arenas in which to test them—and yourself —through trying to reach and persuade others to think as you do. In almost no other setting can one derive such a sense of accomplishment and personal power.

Assessing the full personal meaning of work in public affairs, Mark S. Matthews, author of a major *Guide to Community Action* (1954), states:

> . . . Men and women characterized by leadership qual-
> ities, skills, and knowledges do not appear full-fledged in a
> community, state, or nation. Frequently they are average
> individuals who have grown to leadership stature through
> the practice of leadership in cooperative effort. Through
> group action they have received the human-relations
> understandings and skills necessary to achieve personal
> success, and to make important contributions to their
> community, state, and nation.
>
> · · · · · ·
>
> In addition to enabling individuals to make important
> contributions to our democracy, and to achieve material
> success, organization training and practice bring other
> rich personal returns. There is the extension of self in an
> ever-widening circle of friendship. There is the fulfillment
> of personality, integrated in service to others. And, finally,
> there is the strengthening of character as the developing
> leader responds to the challenge that he exemplify the
> highest ideals of the group. Millions are finding the great
> truth known to philosophers since recorded time; true
> happiness and peace of mind can come only when there is
> a reaching out and an identification of self with others.

To be sure, politics is full of small matters which take time and trouble. But it is also in small matters that some of the greatest rewards may lie. In *Adventures in Politics* (1954) the late Senator Richard L. Neuberger of Oregon has recalled some of his and his wife's moving experiences while both were simultaneously members of the Oregon legislature.

I look back upon a letter I have received from a chief

of upper Columbia River Indians, when no other legislator would champion a resolution urging protection of their treaty fishing rights.

. . . . . .

I can see the stalwart Negro athlete who felt that the civil rights law passed by the Legislature finally assured him the right to eat "down-stairs" in the dining rooms of hotels with his white teammates. He had tears of gratitude in his eyes.

. . . . . .

And I cannot forget the hard-boiled waitress, with two small children, who kissed Maurine's hand because the baby-sitting bill would let her deduct $60 a month before paying the state income tax.

When asked whether much of his work wasn't dull and humdrum, the distinguished Robert Moses, then Chairman of the Power Authority of the State of New York and head of too many other government agencies to catalog them all here, replied with the following.

"There's nothing dull," I told my friend, "about keeping impoverished families from breaking up, about fighting to halt an epidemic of polio, about damming streams and impounding water for reclamation, power, flood control, navigation, and other purposes. There's nothing dull about locating, laying out, financing, and building a housing development which will replace slums, or building great crossings like the George Washington and Triborough Bridges and the Rapid Transit and vehicular tunnels and their arterial approaches and connections in New York City, making possible a civilization which more and more runs on wheels."

3. CONCLUSION

You are not likely to make a fortune in politics any more, and it is sometimes hazardous work in terms of what it may do to reputation and livelihood. But, as Woodrow Wilson said years ago, nothing which is human is alien to politics. Therein lies much of its great attraction.

Read only a few pages about the lives of people like Moses, Neuberger, Fiorello LaGuardia, Mrs. J. Borden Harriman, Ralph Bunche, James M. Farley, Edward J. Flynn, Richard M. Nixon, and James M. Curley (who entitled his memoirs *I'd Do It Again*)—not to mention both Roosevelts, Truman, Eisenhower, L.B.J., and any of the Kennedy clan—and you will gain very quickly a sense of that complex and kaleidoscopic interplay of people, ideas, and institutions which has provided the lure of a life of political action through recorded history. Most of those dipping into the world of public affairs have come back for more.

Chapter 4

How to Get Started

Let us assume you are convinced—that you wish to take some sort of an active part in politics. In recent years it has been fashionable to suggest that the novice should start with precinct work. The precinct *is* a first rate place to begin, but it is by no means the *only* place. Therefore, let us consider alternative ways to begin, and things for the beginner to know, including:

1. *private ways to political influence,* emphasizing the "lone wolf" route, followed by
2. *the "organization" routes,* especially those within the political parties, including
3. *the special case of the precinct,* plus various tips on what to know and how to behave, involving
4. *the role of parliamentary procedure,*
5. *the need to know election law,* and
6. some *other do's and don't's.*

1. PRIVATE WAYS TO INFLUENCE

What Robert E. Merriam and Rachel M. Goetz, in their book, *Going Into Politics*, have termed "private ways of exerting political pressures" are the simplest for the beginner. Some of them may involve no one but yourself. Moreover, while some skills are involved, they are likely to be those you already possess.

1. *Face-to-face contact* is one of the best means to political influence, especially if you are a constituent of the politician with whom you are talking. Beware of threats or verbal bludgeoning, for these may backfire. But a forceful expression of concern or interest, courteously expressed, will almost always receive careful attention. This is especially the case if the politician knows you to be someone of standing, who usually knows what he is talking about. He will usually listen carefully even if your only influence is your own vote. After all, one of the main functions of a politician is to represent his constituents, and to do so he must have some idea about the things in which they are interested. If you can not see him in person, at least try a phone call.

2. *Petitions* are often used by groups of private citizens who wish to bring their names—and their personal views—to bear on a particular issue or candidacy. Petitions may either be sent privately or used as a vehicle for obtaining publicity. In recent years there have been, for example, a large number of petitions on various aspects of war and peace, civil rights, and the use of nuclear energy. But, to be most effective, petitions are usually reinforced by demonstrations and rallies (about which more in Chapter 11) or by—

3. *Personal letters or statements of position.* On occasion, these may have considerable influence, especially if the names of the signers are well known and their views well presented. Sometimes a group of individuals may get together and design a so-called "open letter," addressed either to the person or government agency from which they wish action or simply

to the public in general. An "open letter" is not really a letter, but a public relations device.

Or one may simply write a private letter to a legislator or other political representative. The Democratic National Committee's *Tips for Writing Your Representative* will help insure that your letter has maximum impact.

> Do spell your representative's name correctly and know whether he is a senator or representative.
>
> Do describe the bill by number or by its popular name. Your representative has hundreds of bills before him during the session and cannot always take time to figure out which one you mean.
>
> Do present a concise statement of the reasons for your position, particularly if you are writing about a field in which you have specialized knowledge. Some of the most valuable help your representative can get comes from facts presented in letters from persons who really know what they are talking about.
>
> Do make your letters short.
>
> Do time your letter to arrive while the issue is still alive.
>
> Do write when you endorse the stand your Congressman has taken as well as when you disagree with it.
>
> Don't write your representative more than once on the same subject. Quality, not quantity is what counts.

If you want to promote a mass "letter writing campaign," then two suggestions by Merriam and Goetz are crucial. First, remember that "masses of identical messages are a dead giveaway that the letter campaign was inspired by some interested group." Therefore, direct all concerned "to put the message in the correspondent's own words."

4. *Letters to the editor.* These require some skill, for editors can seldom print all the letters that come to them. They will normally print none that is anonymous or scurrilous. If you request, they will usually delete your name from the printed version. Read the letters in your home town paper for ideas on how to do this. Many of the Democratic National Committee's "tips" above apply here too.

5. *Attendance at open hearings.* Most public agencies are required by law to permit public hearings of proposed actions. Too few citizens attend these hearings, and fewer still attempt to speak. No wonder that public officials are often at a loss as to how to interpret public opinion. However, turning a public hearing to the advantage of your cause is not easy. It takes careful preparation on the issue at hand, together with a well-reasoned and forcefully delivered presentation. Naive, half-cocked remarks spouted forth in the heat of anger will do more harm than good.

6. *Participation in the activities of a private group which has political interests.* Many trade associations, business organizations, unions, farmers' organizations, professional groups, and the like, have interests in political affairs, some regularly and others from time to time. Persons who engage professionally in attempting to influence legislative bodies and other governmental agencies on behalf of special interest groups must often follow certain legal requirements and register as "lobbyists." But most interest groups also need the help of many other individuals to serve on committees, conduct research, make public speeches, design position statements, testify before governmental bodies, and so on. Here too, this kind of activity takes careful preparation if it is to be effective. However, it may permit you to capitalize on special knowledge and abilities you already possess as a member of one of these groups.

2. THE "ORGANIZATION" ROUTES

Here the term "organization" refers to groups whose principal aims and goals are political. Some years ago James A. Farley, former Democratic National Chairman and one of the master political organizers of our time, observed: "The first step in organizing others is to organize yourself." Part of what Farley meant by this has been spelled out by Gus Tyler, director of the political and education departments of the International Ladies' Garment Workers' Union, in *Guide to*

Politics—1954, prepared under the auspices of the Americans for Democratic Action. Tyler's remarks apply equally well today.

There are three kinds of decisions you will have to make about your personal political activity. You may not be able to make up your mind without first sampling and tasting. But here are the decisions you must ultimately make about the nature and degree of your participation:

1. Do you want to get into a party or work through a nonpartisan organization? Many people do both: the party to conduct elections; the nonparty organization to push ideas.

2. Do you want to get into a *permanent* organization or an *ad hoc* organization, thrown together for a given campaign or candidate? It's often easier to get into and to rise in an *ad hoc* organization than in a party where an encrusted leadership has developed. A party offers greater permanence and continuing effort. Many use *ad hoc* organizations as a training ground for party politics.

3. (a) Do you want to take on leadership and party responsibilities, or (b) do you wish to be given a fixed assignment with limited responsibility, or (c) do you just want to help out? It will help you if you know. It will also help the organization with which you are working.

For some of the pros and cons relating to these kinds of decisions, see Chapter 2. The following discussion by Senator Hugh D. Scott, Jr., Republican from Pennsylvania, in his book, *How to Go Into Politics* (1949), should also help.

Making a start in politics as a [precinct] committeeman isn't the only way. You could begin by service on the speaker's bureau in a political campaign, for example. If you do, a national campaign involving a presidential election offers the best opportunity, because the need for and receptivity to volunteers is at the peak. . . . if you have ability as a speaker, as a solicitor of campaign funds, or as an administrator or organizer, here is an opportunity for you to get in the swim where the water is warm and inviting.

Go to the chairman of the political committee or to the chairman of the speaker's bureau or finance committee, tell him what you think you can do, get an assignment, and show all and sundry that you can do it. Don't wait too long to apply; there are usually more offers to help than can be handled. Go in the early organizational stages and if you are given the brush-off try again. Return with reinforcements, such as a phone call or letter of recommendation from someone well known to the chairman. Be prepared to be given routine or pedestrian assignments at first. Count on doing an outstanding job as the best route to more interesting work and a greater share in political activity. If your offer to help in the campaign is accepted and you are thereafter given no work to do, something is wrong somewhere. Go to the chairman and tell him so; if this doesn't work, go to the general chairman in that community. If you have ability, he will be glad to use it; that's why he was put there, to get the best results out of the most people. But don't expect miracles. Expect to be told that you can do your best work on your own street, among your neighbors. You won't be *Mr. Smith Goes to Washington* in your first role. That's just Hollywood again.

· · · · · ·

You will find that, where independent voters' organizations exist, in addition to the regular party organizations, you will usually be welcomed into membership as an independent, if you so desire. Your rise to recognition may seem to be somewhat more rapid than in the more rigidly constituted party organizations. Also, if you have aggressiveness and color, you may find yourself in a fairly short time an independent candidate for some elective office. All of this may look like the royal road to political eminence, . . . but there is a catch to it. . . . you aren't likely to be on the winning side in many elections. Independent movements usually fail through lack of continuity, grassroots organization, and political know-how. Their occasional successes over the major political parties occur at moments of intense public reaction against one or both of the latter.

One of the most complete lists of possibilities for the beginner in political action has been compiled by the U.S. Chamber of Commerce as part of its "Action Course in Practical Politics." Most of the Chamber's suggestions apply equally well to work within the parties or outside them.

Checklist of Political Opportunities for Individuals

CAMPAIGN WORK

Publicity; public speaking; arranging speaking engagements; speech writing; research; legal; filing; typing; making phone calls (to encourage people to register and vote); distributing literature; planning and putting out mailings; manning sound truck; preparing posters, streamers, etc.; putting up posters; designing buttons, car stickers, etc., buying time and space in advertising media.

MEETINGS, RALLIES, SOCIAL EVENTS

Planning programs; planning and running money-raising dinners; acting as Master of Ceremonies; ticket selling; bookkeeping (receipts and expenditures); planning and running a rally; decorations arrangements; organizing parades; obtaining speakers; briefing speakers; escorting speakers to meeting places.

PRECINCT WORK

Preparing voter index cards and lists; phone calls to get people to register and vote); house-to-house canvassing; recruiting party workers; providing transportation to polls on election day; poll clerk; registration clerk; poll watcher; registration watcher; block captain; precinct leader.

ADVANCED WORK

Ward chairman or leader; town chairman or leader; county chairman or leader; campaign manager; finance chairman, publicity chairman, etc.; serving in an appointive government office; candidate for office.

The above list has, however, at least three major omissions. The first has to do with *financial contributions*. Money talks in politics as well as anywhere else, and to contribute to a campaign is often to double the effectiveness of your voice in organization affairs.

The second has to do with taking part in your *local political caucuses*. Caucuses are simply meetings of the members of political organizations, called for the purpose of deciding on policies, for the election of local party officials, or for recommending individuals for nomination to public or party offices. Such caucuses may also select delegates to various party conventions. It is the precinct or other local caucus which provides the real grass roots control of much of our local political activity in this country. For more information about how caucuses work, see Chapter 5. Bear in mind that you do not need an invitation. All you have to do is just go. The rest will take care of itself. Here you can play an important role even if you decide to take little part in other kinds of political activity.

The third possibility involves membership in a *political club*. Until recently the political club was found mainly in the East. The Tammany Hall organization in New York City has for decades consisted of a network of district political clubs. As independent voting became more common after World War II and as shifting groups of like-minded voters sought some means other than the traditional party mechanisms for getting together on particular issues or candidates, the club device spread more widely. Today you will find clubs which are permanent adjuncts or affiliates of the major party organizations, but there are also many which are largely independent.

Obviously, joining a club is a relatively simple way to start in politics. For the beginner there is psychological safety in numbers. Moreover, the club serves as a training ground where one can see and hear about political action before having actually to undertake it. For more about political clubs, see Chapter 6.

Finally, let us consider "the beginner" in the formal party organizations. One of the best summary guides comes from the current outline of a *School for Politics* published by the Democratic National Committee.

Tips for Beginners in Politics

There is no magic formula for "getting active in politics." We can't tell you how, overnight, you can become a delegate to a national convention, or how you can quickly penetrate to the party's inner councils. We can, however, start you on your way. How far you go depends to a large extent on your patience, your persistence, and your willingness to work.

JOIN

Logically enough, you must first join a political party. . . . but it is hard for these groups to find you—so you go to them.

ATTEND

Be faithful in attending precinct, ward, county, district, state, and club meetings. Take part in discussions if you have something to contribute, but don't monopolize the floor. Don't be discouraged if your first efforts aren't welcomed with open arms. Don't try to "take over"—even if you think you can do things better than they're being done. Long-time members of a club or other political group naturally feel a proprietary interest in the group. They may have good reason for not wanting to change to new ways of doing things. But don't give up either. Be polite, patient, and persistent!

VOLUNTEER

The willing political worker is a treasure who soon finds a choice place in the political setting. Volunteer for all kinds of work: typing, ringing doorbells and talking to people about candidates, distributing literature, staffing a campaign headquarters. Many political groups have special committees on legislation, on education, etc. Volunteer to serve on them. If you make worthy contributions, you may soon find yourself a committee chairman— your first step toward political leadership.

INITIATE

If your group does not provide adequate training in political techniques and on issues, offer to help organize techniques workshops and issues discussion sessions. You can get help from other political groups, from your state committee and from the national committee.

SUPPORT

To the extent you can, support your party financially. Some clubs have dues but many do not. Even if your group does have dues to finance its regular activities it can always use more money. You can propose and help to put on fund-raising activities. You can encourage others to contribute to the party. Remember: The more individuals who contribute to a political party, the less chance there is that any one interest group will control it.

PARTICIPATE

As a working member of a political party you can have a voice in the selection of delegates to county, state, and national conventions and a voice in the selection of candidates. Always be on hand to help choose the best representatives possible. As a good worker, you, too, have a chance to be chosen.

3. THE SPECIAL CASE OR THE PRECINCT

"No, starting as a committeeman or precinct captain isn't the only way," writes Senator Scott, but "all things considered, it is probably the best way." Why is this so?

First, a great many elections are, in fact, won in the precincts. But more important from the standpoint of a person who wishes to enter politics is the vast number of workers required to man the precincts. A precinct is merely the generalized name for a single election district, the vote of which is handled and recorded as a single unit. In the late forties there were perhaps 140,000 precincts. With our increase in population, the number of precincts reporting in a national election has grown from over 166,000 in 1960 to more than 175,000 in 1964.

Most precincts contain from 300 to 600 voters, though size

may vary from 200 to 2,000. For each precinct both major parties (plus minor parties in some areas) need a precinct captain or committeeman, plus anywhere from one to ten assistants (often called "block workers") and perhaps a committeewoman. All told, we are talking about a requirement, for each party, of half a million or more workers at the precinct level alone. In many areas the parties are hard put to supply these workers and your help will be most welcome.

Finally, the precinct is a good place to begin precisely because it is one of the smallest of the election districts, sometimes comprising only a few blocks. This small area is easily within the personal reach and knowledge of the beginner who lives there. In your precinct you have the great advantage of knowing the voters in a way that no one else can duplicate. Starting in a precinct simply means that you are using a well-tested formula of success—namely, you are commencing with what you know best.

Now then, *how do you break into precinct work?* Senator Scott's pointers on this procedure are extremely helpful.

> . . . division [precinct] committeemen are usually elected by the voters of the same political party resident in the division. In those localities where this is not the case, selection may be made by a party committee or convention. In any event, the technique of getting started is the same. There may already be a vacancy in your division; inquiry in the neighborhood or at the local political headquarters or club will soon get you this information. If there is, and you want to be considered for the vacancy, go direct to the leader of your ward (or comparable political unit) and tell him so. Tell him things about yourself and why you want to get into politics. He is rather likely to welcome your offer and to undertake to propose your name for the vacant place. The very fact that there is a vacancy is some indication that the ward leader may have been looking around for someone competent to fill it.
>
> Perhaps you will find that in your neighborhood both committeemen are very much on the job and have no present intention of resigning or moving away. In that

case don't decide to retire from politics for the present. The turnover in committeemen is always considerable; meanwhile, there is work you can be doing. Talk to the leader of the ward anyway, and ask him to introduce you to the present committeemen or committeewomen. Tell them you want to help them in the division and ask them to let you work with them in getting out the vote on election day, or in working at the polls. Some committeemen are jealous of their prerogatives and will discourage this. If this happens, you can still do volunteer work at the polls on your own, thus getting acquainted with the voters, or you can take to the side lines, meanwhile improving your acquaintance in the neighborhood, and wait for a vacancy or for the election of new committeemen, at which time you can file for the nomination. This is a simple procedure, in most states requiring only the signature of a few of your neighbors on a petition. Then you can square off to fight it out with the incumbents. This will give you valuable experience—and helpful bumps perhaps—and if you are willing to talk personally with enough of your neighbors, you have a good chance to win the first time around. If both the present committeemen are well known and popular, you may not make it on your first try, but you have already made yourself known to a number of people who will provide a nucleus for your next effort. Actually, one of the present committeemen is likely to be superior to the other and you may nose out the less popular or less efficient one.

Most committeemen will welcome rather than discourage your offer to help. They will need helpers at the polls, watchers (who are designated to protect the interest of candidates or parties), and election officials, such as judges and inspectors of election. They may also need clerks to assist in the registration of voters. . . .

Above all, don't be hesitant about trying to sell yourself, But also be prepared to carry through. Nothing is worse than talking big and then not delivering. Before you start knocking on doors to get into politics, think through your ideas and have a plan. Then present it to someone you feel would be

interested in your efforts—just as you would try to sell anything else. Then get to work and produce.

4. THE ROLE OF PARLIAMENTARY PROCEDURE

In preparing for political action, a good deal depends on
where you are and with whom you are working. But on one
requirement there is complete agreement everywhere. That is,
if you are going to go the organization route, you sooner or
later must learn something about *parliamentary procedure*. At
least a modest working knowledge of *Robert's Rules of Order
for Deliberative Assemblies*, or some comparable set of rules
(there are many such), is a must.

Almost all organizations follow some set of parliamentary
rules, and if one hopes to influence public meetings or to take
a full part in public discussion he must be familiar with these
rules. Nothing is worse than the chairman of a meeting who
lets the discussion get out of hand because he or she doesn't
know what to do.

In addition to knowing some of the "rules," be sure that
you understand such things as (1) the proper order of business, (2) the duties of the secretary and the chairman and
committee heads, (3) the proper way to introduce a speaker,
and (4) how to close a meeting. You should also be familiar
with the constitution and by-laws of your own organization.
You don't have to become a hair-splitting expert on parliamentary detail, but it is absolutely necessary that anyone concerned with organizations know his way around.

This is true even if you never once run a meeting yourself.
For one of the ways that Communists, and other individuals
who are out to disrupt a political meeting, can do the most
damage is by getting things into a parliamentary tangle and
uproar. Some persons specialize in procedure hoping that they
can mix you up or get you sufficiently discouraged with democratic processes that you will give up and go home, thus
turning the meeting (and the organization) over to them.

Be at least smart enough to realize what is being done to you in this kind of situation, and learn enough procedure to support your friends. The best way to battle someone who wants to be difficult about procedure is to know more about it than he does.

5. THE NEED TO KNOW ELECTION LAW

The next requirement—also especially relevant if you choose the "organization route"—is to learn something about *election law*. Most election law is state law. Normally this law is codified and available, usually free, for popular distribution in the form of a booklet or pamphlet. The secretary of state at the state capital usually supplies these. Sometimes the state party organizations also provide summaries of state election law. In larger cities check also with either the city and county clerks or the local board of election commissioners.

Some election law derives, however, from federal action. Here there are two items of special significance—the Federal Corrupt Practices Act of 1925 as amended and the Hatch Act of 1939 as amended. The former regulates the amount of money which may be spent in campaigning for federal office, prescribes how money received shall be accounted for, and prohibits certain kinds of political contributions—especially from corporations and labor unions.

The Hatch Act applies to all federal employees except the top administrative officials and to most state and local government officials who are paid in full or in part from federal funds. The law forbids these officials to engage in active partisan political work while holding appointive office. The ordinary citizens need worry about the Hatch Act much less than the Federal Corrupt Practices Act, but he should be aware of both. The national and state headquarters of the parties can usually supply copies of these statutes.

Of particular interest to the ordinary citizen are the registration and voting laws of the state in which he claims residence. More important to the budding politician are such things as the rules governing the conduct of elections, the filing of nomination petitions, the limitations on political contributions, and the like.

The best way to study these laws is to get a copy and look them over, taking any questions you still may have to someone familiar with the actual operation of politics in your state. In most communities there will also be a lawyer who has specialized to some extent in election law. Go to him for the really knotty problems.

6. OTHER DO'S AND DON'T'S

While politics varies considerably, there are some general principles of good political behavior. Many of the most important have been underscored by Raymond Moley, author, columnist, and former political adviser to Franklin D. Roosevelt, in his pamphlet, *The Political Responsibility of Businessmen.*

How to Behave in Politics—The Individual

Here are a few personal suggestions, proved and tested, for those who want to be an influence in political life:

1. "*Good manners,*" was the instant reply of the most intelligent woman politician of her time, Ruth Hanna McCormick Simms, when a college student asked her, "What is it that makes a good politician?" By this she meant not merely adherence to the strictures of Emily Post. She meant warm concern for the rights, convenience, and dignity of others; that agreeable manner which keeps the other fellow's concerns in the foreground. Politicians must remember that the people whom they seek to persuade are thinking of their own interests. They generally don't give a hang for what happens to the people who solicit their cooperation.

2. *Politics is many little things:* "Let me first be faithful in those things that are least, then I also will be faithful in much."

On another occasion I said this in commenting on the

simple, off-hour interests of Franklin D. Roosevelt, those interests which came to be so well understood to the generality of Americans—an understanding which was a major factor in his prodigious popularity:

"To a philosopher, a scientist or a great lawyer, the preoccupations of a politician seem to be the interests of a person too lazy to apply himself to serious things. This is a gross underestimation of the politician's quality of mind. For beneath the surface he is applying his mental faculties to' exceedingly complex subject matter. Political genius is the capacity to give continuous, undivided, sedulous attention to matters that to most people seem too trivial to bother with."

3. *Be articulate.* Get into community discussions. Take part in forum discussions. Lose no appropriate opportunity to state your views on fundamental political questions. However, this articulation must be kept within the limits of good sense and good taste. Don't be a nuisance.

4. *Be a good neighbor.* Join and be active in local clubs and associations. Throw away the carpet slippers. The best potential that a person can have for exercising political influence is a name well and favorably known in those community activities which have nothing to do with politics. The community is held together with many ties, only one of which is political.

5. *Get your facts straight. Don't be dogmatic.* One of Aristotle's most profound observations was that "anyone is your judge whom you have to persuade."

6. *Don't underestimate yourself.* A character in "The Green Pastures" said, "I ain't much but I'm all I got." The famous George Washington Plunkett of Tammany Hall advised the beginner in politics, "Git a followin', if it's only one man." Remember T.R.'s injunction: "Do what you can, with what you have, where you are."

Moley's advice is applicable to almost any kind of civic endeavor. For recommendations directed toward the party worker, see the following from *You Should Be a Politician* (1959) by Joseph J. Eley and F. Clifton White. These are professional consultants on civic and political organization who have operated under the name of Public Affairs Counsellors,

Inc., of New York. As a personal adviser to Senator Gold-water, White had much to do with Goldwater's capture of the Republican National Convention in 1964.

What you can do

Some do's and don't's that might prove of use to the neophyte going into politics:

Determine which party is most acceptable to you. Don't expect either party to reflect perfectly your philosophy, but choose the one in your locality which is most for the things you feel are right.

Register and identify yourself as a member of the party.

Study the election code of your state, particularly those sections which apply to the formation and operations of the party.

Vote in primary elections, attend precinct caucuses and town, city and county meetings of the party.

Speak up—when you know what you are talking about. When you speak, be guided by the facts and not by anger.

If the leadership of your political party generally reflects your thinking and is honest and efficient, support it to keep it that way.

Don't buck the "organization" unless you have enough votes to defeat it. If the party leadership isn't what you think it should be, build up your faction's strength before you engage in a contest for leadership.

Don't be arbitrary or rigid in your thinking; this doesn't mean that you should compromise principles. There are many ways to climb a mountain. Find a way acceptable to the majority to achieve your objectives and implement your principles.

Don't talk too much. Remember, many people think the wisest man is the man who listens to their ideas.

7. CONCLUSION

At the very least, why not take a good look at your own contribution to the world of political action and see where you stack up.

Here is what might be termed "a minimum check list." It

is part of a one-page broadside once put out by the department of government affairs of the Chamber of Commerce of the United States.

Citizenship Check List

√ Are you a registered voter?

√ Did you vote in the last primary? In the last general election?

√ Do you get out and work for your political organization?

√ Do you maintain close contact with your local public officials?

√ Have you ever offered to serve in public office, or on any public board or commission?

√ Do you know your elected representatives in Congress? Do you write, call, or talk in person with them, and let them know your views on important national issues?

√ Do you keep yourself thoroughly well informed on current public questions?

√ Do you make it a point to find out how your elected representatives vote on important legislation?

√ Do you discuss community and national affairs with the editor of your newspaper, the program director of your radio station, your minister, employees, and school teachers?

Chapter 5

Getting
Organized

Any type of cooperative endeavor requires organization. It is not by chance that the working party structure is known as *the organization*.

Yet, so often it is in organizational matters that the beginner in politics, the political amateur, and even the professional fall down. Politics is constantly a matter of explanation, discussion, education, and salesmanship. All these demand systematic planning and effort, of a simple nature in some situations and more complicated in others.

This chapter deals mainly with what may be termed *regular party organization*. The precinct and county levels are especially emphasized, as these provide the basic building blocks of the state and national party organizations. However, the organization structure outlined here is also applicable to the ward, city, congressional district, or state legislative district levels. Moreover, much is relevant to the organizational problems of independents, union political action groups, and other forms of civic enterprise. All types of political activity require somewhat similar organizational processes.

Do not be intimidated by what follows here. If you are running for village trustee, for the school board in a small district, or for the city council in a community of modest size you will not require anything like the full mechanism described here. Simply read the chapter for ideas which are applicable to your situation. It may be that all you need are some mimeographed handouts (run off by a friend), a literate wife, a friend or two, and ten dollars for postage. Even less "apparatus" than this will do in some cases. But, if you are working within the party organization in a populous district, you will need to know much more.

More specifically, in this chapter we will consider the following:

1. the *political caucus*, the most basic form of political meeting,
2. *block and precinct work*,
3. *county organization*, and
4. the management of a *political headquarters*.

1. THE POLITICAL CAUCUS

Underlying all political organization is the *caucus*. This is simply a meeting of party members. The most fundamental type of caucus, and that dealt with almost exclusively here, is the precinct caucus, representing the smallest of our political subdivisions. This is where party organization begins.

State laws vary in outlining the functions and powers of precinct caucuses. In some states the caucus nominates and elects the precinct leader and approves precinct organization and policies. In most states, however, the powers of a caucus, while still considerable, are mainly advisory to a precinct leader who is elected in a primary rather than by the caucus. Nevertheless, in many areas these caucus meetings are the real sources of party strength, for they represent the hard core of party workers, those who are regularly willing to give of their time and energy. In turn, these workers, by controlling these local meetings, control the grass roots of the party.

Normally any person who is a member of a political party is entitled to attend the caucus of that party. And in some states it is possible to move from the caucus of one party to the caucus of another, provided—as in Massachusetts—"no person having voted in the caucus of one political party shall be entitled to vote or take part in the caucus of another political party within the twelve ensuing months."

In some states the calling of the local caucus is governed by state law, and the procedure to be followed during the caucus meeting is regulated in some detail. In others the party constitutions or other party rules are controlling. Most typically, the caucus is controlled by a combination of law, party rule, and custom.

If you are in doubt about the proper procedure, a phone call to the local election officials or local party headquarters will very likely provide you with the information you want. At the very least you can find out the extent to which precinct caucuses are operative in your area, their powers, and the date of the next meeting for which you are eligible. In any event, and whatever your political aspirations, you should take one in just for the experience.

Now, then, what may go on in a caucus?

Here, for example, is some of the procedure followed in one series of caucuses within the Democratic-Farmer-Labor party of Minnesota.

Democratic-Farmer-Labor
District (Precinct) Caucus Procedure

This brief statement of procedure for the district (precinct) caucuses was written to aid the precinct chairman in conducting their meetings and making the required reports. . . .

NOTICE REQUIRED FOR CAUCUS

By April 25 a copy of the notice of DFL county convention and precinct or district caucuses must be posted on the precinct (township) polling place. The precinct (township) caucus will be held on May 2, between 8 and 9 P.M. (The county-wide publication of this notice is taken care of by the county chairman.)

ASSEMBLING FOR THE CAUCUS

At 8 P.M. on May 2 everyone desiring to take part in the precinct (township) caucus should assemble either at the precinct (township) polling place, or at some other designated place within the district provided that the *Notice of Adjournment* is posted promptly at 8 P.M. in the precinct (township) polling place giving the location of the meeting.

CONDUCT OF THE MEETING

At 8 P.M. the acting precinct (township) chairman should call the meeting to order. The assembled group should then elect by voice vote a new precinct chairman to preside. The next order of business is to elect by voice vote two judges and a clerk who will act as a canvassing board. The specific job of the judges and clerk is to conduct the election of the delegates to the county convention.

• • • • • •

VOTING ON DELEGATES

Voting for the delegates to the county convention must be by written ballot. Each person voting is entitled to write down the same number of names on his ballot as there are delegate positions to be filled. The delegates receiving the highest number of votes are elected. The voting for delegates must be kept open for a full hour so that anyone coming to the meeting by 9 P.M. is permitted to vote. As each person votes, he should sign all three copies of the *Registration Declaration* on the back side of the *Precinct Record and Report*.

• • • • • •

WHO MAY VOTE

If a person's right to vote is challenged he may only vote if he satisfies the judges and clerk by oath that he "did not vote at the last general election, or (that he) voted and affiliated with the . . . (DFL party) at the last general election and intends to so vote and affiliate at the ensuing election."

There are tricks to the trade too, especially in states and localities where the rules are not so precise and where not so many legal precautions are required. The following "tips" were published a few years ago by the Democratic party in Colorado.

Tricks to look for from the Opposition

1. Holding the caucus at a different place from the one announced as the place of the caucus. If you arrive at the designated place of the caucus and are told the caucus is not being held there or if nobody at all is there, simply hold a caucus on the porch or lawn. Attach an explanatory statement to your caucus returns.

2. Setting the clock forward and holding the caucus before the stated time. If you arrive at the caucus and are told it has already been held, insist upon calling time service. . . . At the appointed time, according to time service, simply hold another caucus (outside if not permitted to do so inside). Follow the procedure outlined, have your minutes certified by the caucus chairman, signed by all present, and take the minutes to the county chairman's office immediately.

3. The chairman may attempt to appoint the delegates to the county assembly. Delegates must be elected, so don't let him get by with that trick; if he refuses to allow you to select them, hold another caucus.

4. Holding the caucus in a back room while you sit waiting in front. Keep your eyes open and don't let this happen to you! So that a caucus is held at the appointed time.

There are, of course, other levels of party meetings, moving usually from the county convention to the district convention and on to the state and national conventions. In addition, there may be, in some states, special conventions such as judicial district, school district, ward, or some other type of special district caucus or convention.

The procedure of these higher caucuses and conventions is basically similar to that of the lesser meetings, with the exception that the parliamentary law and other rules governing them are more rigid and are followed with more formality. If you are interested in such matters, write your party state committee for a copy of, for instance, the state convention rules. They should send them to you or tell you where you can find them. The national party headquarters can provide you with rules for the national conventions.

Taken altogether, these caucuses and conventions are the governing bodies of the great political organizations which control our whole democratic political system. And the individuals who control these party meetings inevitably control the ultimate destiny of you and your country.

Remote and insignificant as they may seem, in many areas the precinct caucuses begin a chain reaction of major importance. They are also easy to attend and provide an excellent starting point for the beginner. Here you need no "organization," only yourself.

2. BLOCKS AND PRECINCTS

Next in line is the all-important precinct organization. The details of precinct work are considered in Chapter 12. But it is useful here to view briefly what is involved in a total precinct effort and how this relates to the next major unit of party organization, that of the county. Of course, there are sometimes intermediate ward, city, or district organizations, but, again, it is the precinct which supports the entire structure.

The general form of precinct organization and its relationship to the county mechanism is clearly shown in a chart from the *Democratic Precinct Handbook*, prepared by the Democratic National Committee and reproduced as Figure 1.

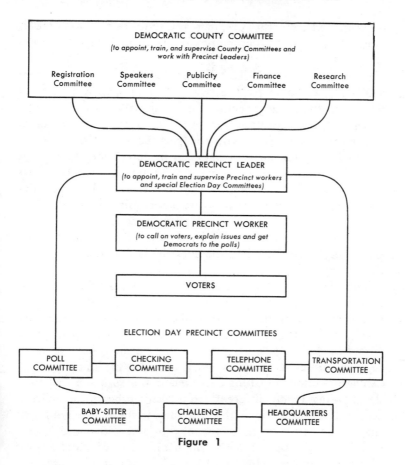

Figure 1

The precinct depends upon the county or larger unit for the more permanent campaign committee work—involving research, finance, publicity, etc. The precinct does not usually have many committees until very close to election time; and those shown here in Figure 1 are typical. In these committees the precinct, in a sense, may duplicate county committees. That is, both political areas may have committees with the same title. However, the county transportation committee is more likely to be involved in a supervisory and emergency capacity, whereas the precinct transportation committee is more directly and continually on the firing line of election work.

Of course, only a fairly large precinct, one involving from 500 to 2,000 voters requires the full organization shown on this chart. In smaller precincts, especially those of 200 voters or less, all that may be needed are the efforts of the precinct leader plus those of his wife and perhaps a few friends.

However, with our rapid growth in population throughout the country, the average number of voters in a precinct has been rising. This means that, for effective work, a precinct leader will in a majority of situations require assistance. This is provided by the precinct worker, better known in cities and metropolitan areas as the *block worker* or, as he is sometimes called, the *visitor*. In the chart he is shown as just above the "voters."

The idea of one person assigned to a particular block has become increasingly popular since World War II. The labor organizations pioneered in this. Block workers are especially involved in personal contact with present and prospective voters in their block, keeping them informed, helping them register, and advising them when they are in difficulty.

The importance of block workers is not so much that they do anything much different from many other local political workers. Rather, it is in the fact that, if there are enough of them, they can do it more thoroughly and with more understanding of the people with whom they are working. A city block—or a comparable rural area—is a manageable unit for one person, who himself is a resident of the area and who knows many of the residents personally. The block idea can sometimes be used to foster a sort of community *esprit de corps* in politics that is otherwise hard to develop in the usual political area whose boundaries may or may not reflect natural group and community interests.

Finally, as both a conclusion to our consideration of precinct work here and an introduction to county organization, let us consider some of the *working relationships* among county, precinct, block, and other local political workers. From a general administrative point of view, *Work and Win!*, a handbook prepared by the Women's Division of the Republican National Committee, provides a useful summary.

The County Committee and the Precinct

The precinct activity follows the campaign plan of the county committee. The county committee, working with the precinct leaders, gives information, inspiration, assistance and direction to the precinct workers. The county committee is the instrument for putting the state committee's program to effective use.

To assist the precinct worker, the county vice-chairman should:

1. Organize training sessions for all precinct workers. Instruct them on registration procedures, filing dates, election laws, issues, candidates, and campaign techniques.

2. Work with nonpartisan groups—enlist the cooperation of every organized group in the county to recruit workers, influence voters, and spread ideas.

3. Hold regular meetings with the precinct leaders to check their progress, discover their needs and give them suggestions. Make them feel that they are members of the team that will carry the banner of Republicanism to victory.

4. Provide speakers for precinct meetings where possible.

5. Give publicity to precinct activities.

6. Make available from the county headquarters the following: digest of laws on registration, absentee voting, rights of polling officials; a calendar of registration deadlines, primary and filing dates; outline of party organization; precinct maps; lists of workers, candidates, office holders, speakers, Republican clubs, nonpartisan organizations, newspapers and radio stations.

• • • • • •

Election timetable. It is helpful if the county committee sets an election timetable. This will serve as a guide to the precinct leaders as to just when certain precinct jobs should be done. Included should be the deadline for:

1. Organizing the precinct—getting block workers, etc.
2. Completing the first and second canvass.
3. Getting all Republican voters registered.
4. Appointing Election Day committees.
5. Naming and instructing election booth officials.

The county committee should prepare an analysis of past voting records, on a precinct basis, for the entire county. This information must be made available to each precinct committee for its use in setting a goal for the precinct campaign.

3. COUNTY ORGANIZATION

Except in very large cities the county is the lowest governmental level at which political organization is relatively complete in terms of the division of labor. Almost all other state and local political entities such as cities, congressional districts, etc., are organized in the same manner as counties. Hence, if you understand county organization, you will have the knowledge necessary for coping with the administrative requirements of most other jurisdictions below the national level.

As noted above, party organization in the county begins with the *county committee*. This is a group of varying size which is usually made up of precinct or other election district leaders known as committeemen. The county committee selects its own chairman, who heads the county political organization and is responsible for its success.

The role of the *county chairman*, a key administrative figure in American politics (about whom even a popular Broadway play has been written), has been briefly outlined by the Democratic State Committee of New York in its *Handbook for Campaign Workers*.

The Leadership

In counties where the party vote is heavy and division of responsibility is necessary, the district, city, or town chairman is a key figure. In counties where the vote is light, the county chairman can assume a more direct share of the work, the blame, and the credit. In either case, theirs is the direct responsibility.

The leader is a man familiar with politics, with the time to devote, on a year-round basis, to the everyday problems of his community and of the party. He is chosen by his committeemen in one sense and, in another, he picks them. He must have lieutenants who are loyal to him, who believe he is doing the job that has to be done. He can influence the selection of committee members, and, in the long run, if they are best for the party, they are best for him. His showing on election day will be on the record, and on the basis of it, appointive party positions will probably be allocated, in addition to the public posts he is able to help the party win.

Party patronage is important in maintaining the party organization. It is sound for the leader to spread around the public positions which are open, or the party favors which are to be granted. Giving everything to a small clique may have two adverse effects. It may foster resentment among those left out. And it may cut down the number of people interested who can be called upon to work in the campaign or at the polls.

The ideal leader is the man who makes the final decision on policy himself, yet who has developed a capable set of lieutenants to guide him in forming that policy and who are equipped to help him carry it out.

Yes, a leader needs support. This comes in the form of a committee structure. In most cases there are three kinds of committees in the county or similar organization: (1) those representing general and continuing campaign functions such as finance, publicity, and research; (2) those which operate almost solely at election time to mobilize automobiles, baby-sitters, and poll watchers; and (3) those formed to cater to special groups such as veterans, women, young voters, and the like.

Our main concern at this point is the first group of committees. The second is discussed in Chapter 13, and the third category in Chapter 6. Nevertheless, it is useful at this point to view county political organization as a whole. A representative pattern, called "County Organization Plan," has been publicized by the Republican State Central Committee of Michigan. It is shown in the next chart, which not only indicates campaign and election committees but also shows the need for liaison with subordinate chairmen and special auxiliary groups.

Of course, in larger counties—indeed, in any heavily populated political unit—it is necessary to divide some functions among several subcommittees. For example, publicity and advertising may be broken down into public relations, advertising, radio and television, and literature preparation. In other situations it may be desirable to coordinate from the top what the Michigan Republicans have termed "local committees." This can add to the list several countywide committees on registration, canvassing, literature distribution, absentee voters, and the like. In addition, special situations may call for a social committee, convention arrangements committee, community service committee, patronage committee, and—most important at particular points in time—a candidates committee.

As for functional coverage, the Michigan chart is reasonably complete except for one major and one minor omission. The major omission is the lack of a law committee. Most political analysts consider a law committee, or some form of legal adviser, to be essential. This is the case with the New York Democratic Committee, which has outlined the duties of a "law committee chairman" in its *Handbook for Campaign Workers*.

> There must also be a *law committee chairman* who will make sure that the party's nominating petitions are properly obtained, are filed in time, and also that the opposition has complied with the full measure of the law. The law chairman should be a man who is in a position to use his legal knowledge to stave off primary election competition which does not meet the election law requirements, or independent candidacies which might adversely affect the party ticket, and to meet all challenges of Democratic

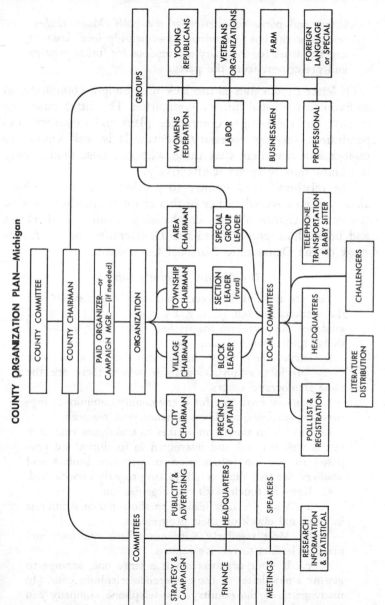

COUNTY ORGANIZATION PLAN—Michigan

COUNTY COMMITTEE

COUNTY CHAIRMAN

PAID ORGANIZER—or CAMPAIGN MGR.—(if needed)

ORGANIZATION

CITY CHAIRMAN — PRECINCT CAPTAIN

VILLAGE CHAIRMAN — BLOCK LEADER

TOWNSHIP CHAIRMAN — SECTION LEADER (rural)

AREA CHAIRMAN — SPECIAL GROUP LEADER

LOCAL COMMITTEES

POLL LIST & REGISTRATION

LITERATURE DISTRIBUTION

HEADQUARTERS

TELEPHONE TRANSPORTATION & BABY SITTER

CHALLENGERS

GROUPS

WOMENS FEDERATION — YOUNG REPUBLICANS

LABOR — VETERANS ORGANIZATIONS

BUSINESSMEN — FARM

PROFESSIONAL — FOREIGN LANGUAGE or SPECIAL

COMMITTEES

STRATEGY & CAMPAIGN — PUBLICITY & ADVERTISING

FINANCE — HEADQUARTERS

MEETINGS — SPEAKERS

RESEARCH INFORMATION & STATISTICAL

Figure 2

voters and party supporters at the polls. Many leaders select for the law committee chairmanship local lawyers eager to work for the party and anxious for future prestige and preferment from the party.

Of lesser significance is the lack of a budget committee, in addition to the usual finance committee. The latter raises the money, but the budget committee plans and completes expenditures, keeping necessary records. It is well known in politics and elsewhere that those who can raise money may not know how to spend it effectively.

The relationships of county to precinct organization have already been covered earlier in this chapter. Another view of the county chairman's job, emphasizing relations both above and below him, comes from the *Democratic County Handbook* of the Democratic National Committee.

The County Leader's Job

You are the link between your state organization and the workers in your county. Everyone looks to you for guidance, support, and inspiration. Here is a checklist of things most county leaders do:

1. Survey the county and see that there is a leader in every precinct, emphasizing those where there are the most Democratic voters.

2. Appoint chairmen for every county committee: registration, speakers, publicity, finance, and research.

3. Meet with these committees to make sure that each one is well manned and instructed in its duties and prepared to pass on information to precinct leaders and workers. See that their activities are properly coordinated.

4. Keep in touch with the organization:

    a. Visit precinct leaders to show personal interest in them and check on their progress.

    b. Meet regularly with committee chairmen and precinct leaders to receive reports.

    c. If your organization is a large one, arrange to get out a newsletter or use conference telephone calls. (In many parts of the country, the telephone company can arrange for you to speak with a number of people at once by telephone. Those you wish to speak to must be notified in advance of the day and time of the conference call so that they will be sure to be at home to receive it.)

    d. Send your own reports to state leaders regularly.

5. Plan ahead for election day work.

6. Hold training sessions.

The above item emphasizes election time work. But many county organizations must to some extent function continuously. The same *Handbook* therefore contains suggestions for "off-year" activities.

Between Campaigns

Elections are won between campaigns. Following is a checklist of activities, based on successful practices:

1. Regular meetings help to keep up the cooperative spirit.

2. Public recognition of workers who have done good jobs keeps them active.

3. Discussion of issues in small and large meetings maintains interest.

4. Committees operate the year around:

    a. The registration chairman watches out for newly naturalized citizens; keeps lists of high school graduates and sends them reminders to register as they come of age; keeps his records current as people move in and out of the county. Work to liberalize registration laws is most important between campaigns.

    b. The finance chairman continues to solicit pledges and contributions, . . . and promote fund-raising projects.

    c. The speakers chairman trains speakers and promotes engagements for them.

    d. The publicity chairman publicizes all events as usual.

    e. The research chairman keeps files current to avoid a last minute rush when campaign time comes around again.

    f. Precinct leaders and workers keep their records on the voters up to date; watch out for the welfare of the

precinct; visit newcomers; help with public problems such
as street repairs, recreational facilities; participate in service organizations and in community activities, such as fund
drives, celebrations of patriotic holidays, and other civic
projects.

For recruitment, appointment, training, and other "personnel" procedures for political workers, see the next chapter.
Meanwhile let us close our consideration of general political
organization with a view of "the headquarters."

4. THE HEADQUARTERS

Any political organization must have a place to work in
and from, a place where workers can come or phone or send
other people for instructions and information. This is the
headquarters, the nerve center of the organization.

Basic headquarters functions and administration are well
outlined in the 1964 edition of *The Democratic Campaign
Manual* of the Democratic National Headquarters.

Establishing Headquarters

Every campaign needs a headquarters, a nerve center,
a command post. The private headquarters from which
policy decisions emanate may be separate from the public
headquarters, which is the focal point of campaign activities involving workers and voters. This section of The
Democratic Campaign Manual is concerned with the
public headquarters, be it state, country, community or
precinct.

Ideal political campaign headquarters are in the ground
floor vacant downtown stores in heavily traveled areas,
easily accessible by automobile or public transportation,
which can be attractively decorated.

The headquarters should be obtained rent free, if possible. Real estate agents very often cooperate with a
candidate by loaning him headquarters space rent free or
at a nominal rent for a few months.

Every headquarters should have an office manager. This

is true whether we are talking about a multi-office headquarters for a statewide campaign, or a 12 x 20 foot vacant
store used as a community headquarters.

The duties of the office manager include these:

Recruitment and assignment of volunteer workers. (He
may appoint an assistant, or several assistants, to help him
with this.)

Setting up the work schedule.

Maintaining names, addresses and telephone numbers of
all headquarters personnel and volunteers.

Responsibility for getting out the mail. (Physically, that
is; the office manager should not be expected to dictate
the letters or prepare the statements.)

Responsibility for mimeographing or otherwise repro-
ducing campaign materials.

Obtaining and maintaining sufficient numbers of type-
writers, desks, chairs, and other campaign equipment and
material.

Knowledge of postal regulations, care and operation of
business machines, familiarity with mailing services, sign
companies, etc.

Responsibility for accepting, storing, and distributing
campaign materials.

Depending upon the size of an operation, the office
manager might also be responsible for such activities as
negotiating with printers and sign manufacturers, supervising the erection of signs, and any number of other
activities generated through the campaign headquarters.

*Here are some general rules to observe about deco-
rating and staffing any headquarters:*

Headquarters should be attractively decorated with
Johnson for President signs, other Democratic signs, red,
white and blue bunting and streamers, pictures of the
President and other candidates, bumper stickers, brochures, blown-up photographs, and other campaign materials.

There should be a large sign over the front of the
headquarters, preferably lighted.

Headquarters should be kept as neat and clean as possible, windows should be washed regularly.

The headquarters should maintain a regular work schedule. Nothing is more deadening than a dull, dreary campaign headquarters, with doors locked and no one around.

Supplies of brochures, bumper stickers, buttons, tabloids, biographies, photographs and other campaign literature and materials should be on hand at all times.

Telephones should be answered "Johnson for President Headquarters" or "Smith for Congress Headquarters," or whatever candidate the headquarters is representing, or "Democratic Headquarters" or "Jones County Democratic Headquarters."

Impress upon each volunteer worker who might be answering the phone that, to the caller, he represents the candidate. It is imperative for volunteers, and anyone else answering the phone, to be courteous and polite at all times.

Persons who answer the phone must be impressed with the extreme importance of taking and leaving messages for key personnel who may not be in at the time the call comes in.

When mailings are scheduled the office manager must make certain there are adequate supplies of envelopes and insertions in the headquarters. Few things are more discouraging to a volunteer worker than to go to headquarters, prepared to work, and find that there are no envelopes to stuff or no brochures available.

There undoubtedly will be more than one headquarters in many campaigns. All headquarters should follow the same general rules set forth here.

As for special headquarters and other organizational problems relating to the role of the candidate and his personal campaign manager as opposed to the more permanent party organization, see Chapter 9.

5. CONCLUSION

Actually, no two caucus, precinct, county, city or other political mechanisms will be exactly alike. But, as you can see, there are some standard problems and there will need to be chairmen and committees to meet them. Judge what you need in light of your job and your resources, and organize accordingly.

Chapter 6

Recruiting
and
Training

Some political work will be done by persons who are on the job nearly all the year around. But during campaigns and elections political organizations often expand to several times their normal size. This requires a vast number of temporary and part-time workers to augment the regular staff.

Good organization demands good personnel. Better one good precinct committeeman than three mediocre to poor ones. During campaigns, when long hours and hard work are "musts," it becomes highly desirable to recruit workers in a systematic fashion and to train them well.

Therefore, this chapter is concerned with the *personnel phase* of political organization and action. Specifically, we will consider:

1. *who appoints whom*—that is, who has the power to hire and fire?

2. *the estimating of personnel needs*, plus a general consideration of the probable supply of available talent;
3. *the recruiting of workers* as a general problem;
4. *the recruitment of special groups* representing the varied
interests of young voters, women, businessmen, veterans
and the like; and
5. *the training of workers*, particularly via the growing number of schools of politics and political institutes.

1. THE APPOINTING PROCESS

Someone must be able to hire—and also to fire—workers.
This is true of all organizations. Because any worker in politics
is necessarily also a "customer," the appointing and removal
of political personnel is often a delicate matter.

The matter is further complicated by the fact that the
organizational heads at various levels may be elected. This
means that a county chairman, for example, can not remove
many of his subordinate district heads. His only real opportunity comes when there are vacancies to be filled between
elections. Then the county chairman can usually appoint
precinct, ward, or district chairmen or committeemen.

Fairly typical "personnel" relationships among county, precinct, and block workers have been outlined by the Women's
Division, Republican State Central Committee of Ohio, in
the pamphlet, *"How To" for the Precinct Worker*. In those
states where precinct heads are selected by caucus, substitute
the words "selected through the party caucus" for "elected in
the primary."

Organization

The success of a party organization rests primarily on
the precinct committeeman, the precinct committeewoman, and their auxiliary workers. . . .

The precinct committeeman is elected by the Republicans in his precinct who vote in the primary. The precinct committeewoman is appointed, usually by the pre-

cinct committeeman, with the approval of the county
chairwoman. The county chairwoman is appointed by the
county chairman in most instances. Thus the precinct
committeeman and precinct committeewoman serve as
chairman and co-chairman of a precinct organization,
which organization includes recruits from Women's
Republican Clubs, Young Republican Clubs, Citizens for
Eisenhower groups, nonpartisan men's and women's clubs
and veterans groups.

From the above organization a block system of workers
may be set up, to the end that every home in a precinct
is easily serviced by Republican workers for the Republican cause.

Organize your precinct with volunteers. Impress upon
them the importance of their volunteer work, then give
them a job to do.

That is, the political chairmen or organization heads at any
given level have a good deal of authority over their own
workers at their own level. But such chairmen may have little
or no authority in the hiring and firing of chairmen one or
more levels below them or of workers at levels below them.

Moreover, during elections it is recognized that a party
nominee has a right to considerable say-so over political party
officers and appointments in his campaign area. Otherwise, the
candidate might find some appointees working against him,
or his political enemies receiving preference over his friends.
County, district, state, and national chairmen are especially
subject to a candidate's veto.

Nevertheless, all authorities agree that, once their position
is secure, the chairmen of the various political areas must
have full command in their own bailiwick—that is, in their
own immediate organization. They must especially be given
the power to appoint and to relieve all of their committee chairmen and committee members, any paid employees
whether full or part time, as well as any volunteers. They
may delegate these tasks, but the ultimate authority remains
with the area chairman. In its current *Democratic Campaign
Manual*, the Democratic National Committee recommends that

the "Campaign Director" (synonymous with "chairman" in this discussion) should appoint all committee chairmen and that "no persons should be added to the campaign payroll without the approval of the Campaign Director."

Upon party leaders also falls the job of appointing those who represent the interests of the party during the election day process. The following example comes from *The Way to Win: Success Strategy*, an organization manual prepared by the South Dakota Republican Central Committee.

Appoint Election Officials

Not later than the middle of September—certainly by October—your county central committee should see to it that a list of election officials (judges and clerks) is delivered to the county auditor. *Where Republicans had the majority in the last election, they should have two Republican names as judges in each precinct.* The judges shall designate the clerks in each precinct, except in precincts numbering less than 25 votes in the last election where the judge shall act as clerk. See that good, competent Republican men and women are certified to the county auditor for these positions and get their names in on time.

Pick qualified judges. Make sure they know their duties. This must be an honest election. Hold an instruction conference before election day for your judges and clerks of election.

Finally, after an election it may fall to the party officials—along with the successful candidates—to recommend persons to appointive political office. This is referred to as the distribution of the spoils of victory, more commonly known as *the patronage*. So-called "patronage jobs" usually go to the most conscientious and influential party workers. Indeed, the possibility of elective or appointive office provides one of the major incentives for party workers—particularly full-time workers—in many parts of the country. Many others find party work attractive and interesting for all the other reasons outlined earlier. Actually, patronage as a motivating force for political participation has been declining for a good many

years. Today an increasing number of party workers are
personally interested in candidates and issues more than in
the party as a possible source of employment.

2. ESTIMATING PERSONNEL NEEDS

The personnel requirements of political parties during major
elections are enormous. Conservatively estimated, our two-
party system can easily absorb on a more than casual basis
the services of at least 2,000,000 persons during an election
year, and perhaps two or three times that many. No party has
yet had all the workers it wanted or could use. Such is the
measure of your opportunity for political work.

But what about measures of personnel needs in specific
political organizations below the state level? In its precinct
manual, *Insurance for Winning Elections,* the Republican
State Central Committee of California has recommended that
"for best results in working a precinct, there should be one
worker for each 50 to 75 Republicans, depending largely upon
population density and geographical expanse." Actually, this
ratio is minimal for really good work. In its list of duties for
The District Chairman the Republican State Committee of
Delaware has recently recommended that "ideally, twenty
houses would be as many as you would want to ask one
worker to handle. For example, if you have 600 people in one
district to vote, this would mean about 300 homes, so you
would need 15 workers." Still another rough measure for use
in cities, towns and villages is one person to a block. But,
again, this must vary according to the density of population
per block. If there are many apartment buildings, one person
per block may not be enough.

Another approach has been provided by the National
Municipal League in its booklet, *The Citizen Association:
How to Win Civic Campaigns.*

Volunteers do the Job

Basic committees are finance, speakers, education, candidates, publicity, block organization, telephone, and

transportation. In large cities separate committees for women volunteers, veterans, labor, businessmen, and young people are often established.

Paid staffs are usually found only in bigger cities with campaign budgets of $10,000 or more. Most communities rely on volunteers from top to bottom, unless the campaign is being managed by the full-time staff of a permanent citizen association. It is poor policy to pay block canvassers.

You need 1 percent of the People

Seventeen organizations reported to the National Municipal League on the number of volunteers used in campaigns for council-manager charters or for slates of candidates. The range was from 1/50 of 1 percent of the population to 2 percent, with a median of 1/3 of 1 percent.

A desirable goal is about 1 percent of the population. It will not be a herculean job for the nucleus of committee members to enroll this number if the recruiting process is decentralized. The central committee should select able chairmen for wards or districts, letting the ward chairmen find block workers. Door-to-door canvassing is feasible when 1 percent of the population is working for the campaign.

The League's estimate that "you need 1 percent of the people" to organize a successful civic campaign is equally applicable to almost any kind of civic or political action. This does not mean that you need this many full-time workers. Rather, this kind of criterion refers to your requirement for all kinds of personnel—full time or part time—in all types of positions during the full course of a major campaign.

Still more helpful is the following table from the *Missouri Practical Politics Handbook* prepared by the Missouri State Chamber of Commerce. This contains the most extensive work measurement data now available on political tasks. Bear in mind this table represents experience in an exceedingly populous area which contains 26 precincts.

TABLE 1. Time Required for Party Jobs in One St. Louis County Township

No. of Persons	Job Description	Time Required per Person During a Two-Year Period
26	*Precinct Committeemen* to organize your precinct by blocks. Average 300 homes. Get 1 asst. and five block captains. Help with canvassing. Get ballots distributed to homes. Have every home contacted. Get voters registered. Locate voters. Get them to polls on E-Day. Man the polls with workers. Assist in money raising once every 2 years in house to house canvass. Attend Committeeman's meetings. Get drivers for E-Day. May serve as delegate to State Conventions	6 evenings a year on off year. 2 week ends (Saturday and Sunday afternoons) a year on off year. 6 evenings a year on election year. 4 week ends a year on election year. *Total hours: 102 of 17,520*
26	*Ass't. Precinct Committeemen:* Understudies the Precinct Committeeman and assists in carrying out the duties listed above under his direction. Votes for Pct. Committeeman in his absence on all matters of policy, candidates, etc. Attends meetings in his absence and some with him.	3 evenings a year on both off years and election years. 2 week ends (Sat. & Sun. P.M.) on off years. 4 week ends as above on election years. *Total hours: 84 out of 17,520*
130	*Block Captains:* Keeps in touch with approximately 60 homes or about 3 or 4 blocks in precinct in off year and twice on election year (Primary and General Election). Helps get drivers, polls workers on election years and raise money with house to house canvass.	1 evening a year on off year. 2 evenings a year on election year. 1 week end (Sat. & Sun. afternoon.) on off year. 2 week ends (ditto) on election year. *Total hours: 42 out of 17,520*
52	*Poll Workers:* Works at polls handing out ballots and checking off	No work off years. 2 days election year.

TABLE 1. (Continued)

No. of Persons	Job Description	Time Required per Person During a Two-Year Period
	voter lists on election day. Men usually work early A.M. and late P.M. Women during day unless men can give all day.	*Total hours:* 24 out of 17,520
26	*Drivers:* Available at each precinct on election days to bring voters, get voters, run errands.	No work off years. 2 days on election year. *Total hours:* 24 out of 17,520
6	*Headquarters Chairmen:* One person for each day of week during months of July, August, September, October and 1 week in November. Supervises and helps in clerical work at headquarters.	No work on off years. 14 days during election year. *Total hours:* 114 out of 17,250
26	*Telephone Captains:* Organize and recruit 10 ladies (for each precinct). Each lady to look up 30 telephone numbers and call them on election days. Callers time: 6 hrs./election.)	All work done in August and November of election year only. *Total org. hours:* 20 out of 17,520
75	*Business and Professional Men:* to raise $100.00 each. This is done once every two years.	*Total hours:* 10 (1 call per hr.) ($10.00 per call.)

Translating the above table into the personnel requirements for a single precinct with a large voting population, one comes up with a need for one precinct committeeman and one assistant committeeman, five block captains, two poll workers, one driver, one telephone captain and ten ladies to assist, plus three business and professional men—a grand total of twenty-four (24) workers per precinct. Of course none of these workers is full time, and most function only during the few days or few weeks just before an election.

However, the above data do not take into account the especially hard-fought campaign, or the need in many areas for a corps of "non-working" advisers, contributors, and supporters of various kinds. These are minimum rather than maximum measures of personnel requirements.

3. RECRUITING THE WORKERS—GENERAL

Of course paid workers pose few recruitment problems, and very large campaign organizations at the state, metropolitan and congressional district levels will require some. But, as the Democratic National Committee has put it, "volunteers are the life blood of a campaign." What about their supply and availability?

No one knows precisely. However, a Gallup poll taken January 12, 1956 indicates that there was then an immense "army" of potential volunteers ready and willing to serve the major parties. Apparently close to 10,000,000 were ready to do some active work for the Democrats and 7,000,000 for the Republicans. Nearly as many women as men expressed such a desire. The survey also suggests that there is a great untapped reserve of college-trained potential volunteers. In general, the higher the level of education, the greater the interest in political participation.

All the current evidence would indicate that Gallup's 1956 findings are still relevant. That is, it would appear that there are more than enough potential volunteers to meet the needs, if they are appealed to properly and utilized effectively.

This means following some general rules. These have been precisely and simply laid out by the *Republican Handbook* of that party's New Jersey State Committee.

Volunteers can be Recruited if

1. they are asked.
2. they are given a specific job and plan.
3. they are given a reasonable amount of work.
4. they are shown that they are performing a valuable service.

In implementing these principles, the first warning that should be observed has been well put by the Republican National Committee in its *Campaign Manual* of some years ago.

Don't Recruit until you can put Them to Work

The recruitment of workers should be deferred until an adminstrative framework has been set up which is completely capable of absorbing the workers as fast as they come in. *Nothing discourages a volunteer more than indifferent treatment or having to hang around with nothing to do.* Clear arrangements should be made in advance to channel every volunteer *immediately* into one or more divisions, where he can *immediately* be put to work.

Most volunteers will not know what type of work they prefer, and since canvassing ordinarily absorbs the bulk of volunteers, the best procedure is to channel all such volunteers directly into the canvassing division.

As for sources of volunteers and recruitment procedure, let us look again at the current *Democratic Campaign Manual:*

Volunteers

Volunteers are essential to the success of any political campaign.

RECRUITING

Most candidates can enlist a nucleus of volunteers from their friends and relatives. If they presently are officeholders, or have run for office in the past, they probably have names and addresses of persons who have worked for them before. If the campaign is being coordinated with other Democratic campaigns (as it should be), there may be campaign workers available at state, county and local Democratic headquarters. . . .

There is no such thing as having a surplus of volunteers. There are any number of ways of recruiting volunteer workers, including:

Asking persons who have offered their services to President Johnson and other Democratic candidates.

Asking persons who have returned worker cards (see

next section) indicating they will perform some specific volunteer function in the campaign.

Asking college and high school students.

Asking members of political, civic, church and social clubs.

Asking persons who express a desire for political participation and experience.

Asking persons who have worked in previous political campaigns.

Asking elderly persons, who may be willing to perform light campaign chores, such as addressing envelopes.

Asking members of Democratic state, city, county and town committees.

Asking members of labor unions referred to the candidates by AFL–CIO Committee on Political Education (COPE) or other union groups.

Asking the wives, husbands, sons, daughters, sisters, brothers, fathers, mothers, aunts, uncles, cousins and friends of everyone in the preceding categories.

It is unlikely that all members of a club or civic group will volunteer to work for any candidate. But if lists of members in these organizations can be obtained, a personal call or letter (containing the worker card) should be directed to these potential volunteers.

When the candidate announces, he may wish to send a mailing to selected persons—friends, acquaintances, members of various clubs or unions, or any other lists of persons he feels might be useful to him in his campaign. Included in this mailing should be an appeal for volunteer assistance, with a copy of the worker card.

While mass mailings are not notoriously productive of volunteer workers, a mailing that turns up a handful of good workers, not to mention what other purposes it was intended to accomplish, may well have been worth the effort and expense.

College and high school students are particularly good for leg work—house-to-house distribution, errands, putting up signs, mailing and addressing letters, making phone calls, etc.

Just because a young person is not old enough to vote

is no reason to discourage him from working in the campaign. Many of the Democratic Party's best volunteer efforts come from very young people. High school youngsters, under adult supervision, do a good job working on bumper sticker teams in shopping centers and other areas. (The bumper sticker operation is described in detail later in this manual.)

WORKER CARDS

An effective method of obtaining the names of potential volunteer workers and at the same time categorizing them by the type of work they are willing to do is through use of a *worker card*.

Here is a basic format for the worker card.

YES! I would like to work in the campaign to re-elect President Lyndon B. Johnson. You can count on me to:

☐ Address envelopes   ☐ Raise funds
☐ Distribute literature   ☐ Drive voters to the polls
☐ Work at headquarters ☐ Make telephone calls
☐ Put a sticker on my car ☐ Do typing, cut stencils
☐ Work on a bumper-   ☐ Put up signs
     sticker team   ☐ Deliver campaign material
☐ Make a campaign   ☐ Do anything at all
     contribution   ☐ Us my name in endorsements

Name_____

Address_____

Telephone (Home)_____(Work)_____

Figure 3

These cards should be imprinted with a first class return mail permit, addressed to campaign headquarters. They should be included in all early mailings. Members of the campaign staff should carry some with them at all times.

All headquarters should have a supply. Volunteer workers should be encouraged to ask their friends, relatives, and neighbors to send in a worker card.

It is the responsibility of campaign headquarters to make certain these cards are properly filed—*and that everyone who volunteers to work is given an assignment.*

The Democratic worker card above is typical, except that in many organizations the name and address lines are at the top of the card, thus facilitating filing.

Finally, let us consider briefly *just how one goes about finding workers,* in this case for a precinct. A practical approach has been outlined in the precinct manual of the Republican State Central Committee of California, *Insurance for Winning Elections.*

How to Locate Precinct Captains and Coworkers

Locating or recruiting personnel to serve as precinct captains and their coworkers is, in truth, the crux of establishing an adequate precinct organization. This is where well laid plans may fall down. First, the general precinct chairman recruits as many as possible of his or her precinct captains from the memberships of the several volunteer Republican organizations—the Young Republicans, the Federation of Republican Women's Clubs, the Republican Assembly, members of both the county and state central committees. The appeal to these groups should be pin-pointed to specific precincts, since a general appeal for precinct workers usually results in a large number of volunteers from densely populated areas with the majority of precincts still uncovered. The best way to handle this is to list the precincts by number and opposite the number give one central cross street—i.e., "Precinct No. 342—Broadway and 29th St." Then ask for someone who lives within, say, a block of that cross street.

But, no matter how many recruits are obtainable from the memberships of these official volunteer Republican groups, the chances are the great majority of precinct captains and co-workers will come from the relatively "unknown" *Mary Does* and *Joe Doakes*—that vast army of workers who are politically active only at election time and hold no continuing interest in political work between-times.

The simplest way to reach these people is for the area and division chairmen to check the roster of voters (precinct sheets) in their jurisdiction for names of Republicans whom they may possibly know. Call on them, either in person or by telephone. Then, where the area and division chairmen do not personally know any of the registered Republicans, start telephoning ALL registered Republicans within a precinct until a precinct captain is located. And as soon as possible call upon the prospective precinct captain in person to explain the nature of the assignment. This activity will also turn up good co-workers.

In a recent special election in Sacramento, 280 precinct workers to cover 220 precincts were obtained in this way in four days of telephoning from the precinct sheets! It works—and works well—when begun early enough. After all, the only Republicans who can possibly help the Republican cause are *listed on those precinct sheets*. There are no other voting Republicans available to anyone.

Of course, the technique outlined above is most useful for placing relatively untrained workers into jobs where they may be of most use. But in many respects, this is the most difficult task. Persons with specialized skills—in public relations, for example—are likely to be already known. Even so, it is highly desirable to keep the kind of individual record for each worker recommended in the item just above from the *Democratic Campaign Manual*. Then one is prepared for any emergency requiring special abilities or interests.

4. RECRUITMENT—SPECIAL GROUPS

The use of women, teen-agers, union members, and representatives of similar groups has been mentioned above. Let us consider the problems of recruiting and utilizing "special groups" in more detail. Any campaign, even a small one, will need to channel appeals to such groups. In addition, many useful volunteers will come from their ranks.

We cannot consider all such groups here, nor look at even a few in depth. But we can at least scan the possibilities with certain major types—specifically, those involving young people, women, senior citizens, various important interest groups, and club members.

Although there is an increasing tendency these days for the political parties to court the youth of the land, *young voters*— and other "first voters"—provide a source for working personnel which is often overlooked. The various mechanisms for mobilizing young voters tend to be four in number: (1) first voters campaigns, (2) teen-age clubs, (3) college student clubs, and (4) area young Republican or Democratic clubs which include all between the ages of eighteen and thirty-five.

Actually, the first three types of activity tend to be conducted under the auspices of or in association with the area clubs. As the activities and organization of the young voter groups closely resemble those of the regular party organization, described elsewhere in this book, there is no need to go into further detail here. For literature on organizing and running a Young Republican or Young Democratic or other similar group at the college or "teen" levels and above, write to your party's state or national headquarters. There are model constitutions and bylaws available along with suggested programs of study and action.

Just as important as a source for active political workers are the *women's political organizations*.

The idea of "50–50" (50 percent men to 50 percent women) membership on political committees, required by law in many states and customary in many more, is becoming almost universal. When one considers that the potential vote of women is greater than that of men, the need to integrate women more fully into the political program becomes even more compelling. The stepping up of appeals to the women's vote during the last two decades has become increasingly apparent.

In some areas—notably California—political organizations have occasionally gone so far as to abolish their separate women's divisions, integrating women fully into the campaign organization structure. The most compelling reasons for doing this were summarized in 1955 by Murray Chotiner, who for some years assisted in the campaigns of Richard M. Nixon and others in California. Chotiner, in an address (which is still widely circulated) before the Republican National Committee's Campaign School, said that in the California campaigns which he and his associates had directed they had decided

> . . . to treat the women as equals. You'd be surprised at how well they like that. We found that if a woman would make a better chairman of any of these groups or committees than a man, we appointed the woman as chairman. In all of the campaign organization we had many women who headed up the groups. If we found for any reason we wanted a man to head up the particular function, we always had a woman co-chairman—not a vice-chairman, not a woman who was going to function merely as an adjunct.
>
> Now, the reason it is important in my opinion not to have a women's division is this: If you organize a women's division, they will work among the women in the campaign; and if your male chairman falls flat on his face, and doesn't do anything, you have an entire segment of your campaign that is a complete blank. . . . We found, for example, in one city our chairman really fell flat on his face; he got busy with other things. But we had a woman as co-chairman, she took over the whole thing, and everything was functioning well for our candidate.
>
> So we use the woman as equal to the man in every phase of the campaign.

However, the doctrine outlined above is still much the exception. A more typical arrangement is described in the New

York Democratic State Committee's *Handbook for Campaign Workers.*

The Women

The women's division of the Democratic State Committee is constantly on the alert to find out the issues in which women are interested, to report back to the party's leadership on what steps must be taken to insure that the party gets the same large share of the women's vote at the next election that it received in past elections.

· · · · · ·

The New York State Democratic organization has been fortunate for many years in the close cooperation which has existed between the formal party organization and the women's division.

This is headed by the vice-chairman of the Democratic State Committee, and her contact in each county is the regularly elected county vice-chairman, who is *ex officio* head of the county women's division. In most counties there is also a program director, appointed with the approval of the local county chairman and vice-chairman.

The vice-chairman of the state committee is responsible for the sending out of a continuous stream of educational material, starting with the party's legislative program, and containing suggestions for meeting topics, publicity, and getting out the vote.

Both during campaigns and in the off-season, the women party workers have proven invaluable. Their share in the work and their ability to perform any kind of task have led to increasing recognition in the form of nominations to public office and appointments to public posts.

Details on possible programs and activities are available from the women's divisions of the national and state party organizations as well as from the Women's Activities Department of the AFL-CIO Committee on Political Education and the various Leagues of Women Voters.

Let us now consider other types of auxiliaries, most of which are much less well organized on a national scale than the young people and women. Of increasing importance are organizations of older voters, often termed Senior Citizens Committees. The Democratic National Committee has thus characterized the organization of senior citizens in its *Democratic Campaign Manual.*

Senior Citizens Activities

Senior Citizens—men and women of retirement age— often have much free time on their hands, and can handle many volunteer projects at campaign headquarters.

They should be given physically easy jobs, such as addressing and stuffing envelopes, putting telephone numbers on voting lists, making telephone calls, answering telephones in headquarters, and other similar tasks.

There are more than 17 million persons in the United States over 65 years of age. They represent a vast reservoir not only of potential volunteer workers but also of voters. . . .

In appealing to Senior Citizens for their vote, any candidate should:

Emphasize the close ties between President Johnson and the Democratic Party platform with the needs of the elderly.

Contact every recognized leader of Senior Citizen, Golden Age, and similar clubs to solicit support and endorsement—and don't forget to ask if they'd like to work in the campaign.

Create a committee of Senior Citizens to advise about their particular problems, and to assist in his campaign. He should make sure to obtain maximum publicity from this committee.

Aim some pieces of campaign literature specifically at older persons; emphasize the Democratic Party's position on programs affecting the aged.

Even more important are the organized representatives of various *important interest groups.* Again, the Democratic National Committee has well summarized what is involved in appealing to some of these groups.

Farm Activities

Farmers are among the most politically involved voting groups in the country. Many have determined opinions about the candidates and the issues as related to the welfare of the farmer. Many are members of politically active farmers' organizations.

Lining up workers and votes among farm groups can be a difficult job—but in many states it is an important one, perhaps the key to winning or losing the election.

. . . A farm chairman should . . .

Emphasize the ties between President Johnson and the farmers of America.

Inform farmers of the legislation favorable to farm groups that has been sponsored and advanced by the Democratic Party.

Arrange for the distribution of campaign literature by farm groups and families to farm groups and families.

Make certain that leaders in farm groups have access to the candidate and key campaign officials.

Arrange for appearances by the candidate before farm groups, with opportunities for question-and-answer sessions.

Labor Activities

Organized labor can be a prime source of manpower and, in some cases, campaign contributions for Democratic candidates. The AFL–CIO's COPE (Committee on Political Education) is one of the most effective and best-organized political units in the country.

The candidate, through his labor chairman appointed by the campaign director, should contact the local or state COPE leader and arrange a meeting with him and the key campaign people to determine what assistance organized labor can and is willing to provide.

COPE and international and local union groups often sponsor public meetings for candidates, and many times invite all candidates to appear before an endorsement board to present their cases. In such a case, the candidate should be well briefed on union positions on various, issues, and be prepared to discuss positions intelligently.

. . . . . .

Veterans Activities

Many veterans organizations have active citizenship units and members who are good political workers. Contact should be made with the leaders of all veterans organizations in each area, and a top-flight veteran should be selected to head a Veterans Committee for President Johnson and for the local candidate.

. . . . . .

Business Activities

Democratic candidates sometimes have a tendency to ignore the potential support available to them from businessmen.

. . . Many businessmen do not participate in political campaigns because they never have been asked. The very fact that they are in business can make them extremely valuable in many areas of campaign activity—such as purchasing agent, auditor, or the finance committee.

Creation of a businessmen's committee is a newsworthy item and should be given maximum publicity. Appointments to the committee, endorsements, and other activities also should be publicized.

Professional Activities

Lawyers are among the most politically active persons in the country. Doctors, dentists, architects, nurses and other professional people also should be encouraged to serve on a professional committee and provide whatever other assistance they can to the campaign.

Arrangements should be made to have the candidate address meetings of professional societies and other groups with high professional membership.

These kinds of groups may be organized in one of three ways. They may be tied in directly with the regular party organization. They may be organized parallel to, sometimes even independently of, the parties. Or they may function through some sort of political club system. Let us consider each type briefly.

When formed by the regular party agencies they normally operate under the general supervision of a "special groups chairman" appointed by the county or other area chairman. Such an arrangement is suggested in the *Democratic Congressional Campaign Manual* of 1962.

Special Groups Chairmen

In order to use all manpower resources and involve all citizens in the campaign, efforts will be made to enlist support through specialized groups of voters who might not otherwise become involved in a congressional campaign.

There already have been organized at the national level committees of prominent persons identified with special groups, such as senior citizens, veterans, or young citizens. These national committees have staffs specially trained to help you mobilize these groups to assist your district congressional campaign committee. It is the responsibility of the chairman of the special groups committee to appoint, as he deems appropriate, a chairman for each group. In doing so, he is urged to consult the national representatives of the various specialized groups to insure appointment of suitable persons.

Under such a chairman will be the Engineers and Scientists for Candidate X, the Lawyers for X, the Sportsmen for X, the Artists for X, and so on. At the national level in 1964 the Republicans were reported to have had 28 such "auxiliaries" and the Democrats 22.

The Citizens for Eisenhower groups were an outstanding example of a web of volunteers formed independently of and, in the beginning, in opposition to the regular organization. They were instrumental in 1952 in helping Eisenhower defeat the regular forces backing the late Senator Robert A. Taft of Ohio for the Republican presidential nomination. Similar volunteer citizens groups have been part of all major campaigns ever since. In 1964 the Citizens for Goldwater-Miller and the Citizens for Johnson and Humphrey functioned in a relatively decentralized way. Only a very loose supervision was maintained by the national party headquarters in Washington. This kind of volunteer group activity is becoming increasingly common at all levels of government.

Related types of independent auxiliaries are the AFL-CIO Committees on Political Education (COPE), the political action arms of many of the labor unions. See the latest edition of their excellent handbook for union members entitled *How to Win: A Handbook for Political Education,* available from the central COPE headquarters in Washington, D.C.

Since the middle 1950s there has been some promotion of business equivalents of COPE. On these developments, see J. J. Wuerthner's *The Businessman's Guide to Practical Politics* (Chicago), revised 1961 edition; *Politics Is Your Business* by William H. Baumer and Donald G. Herzberg (New York), 1960; and *Politics and the Businessman* by David J. Galligan (New York), 1964.

Finally, there are the *political clubs,* mentioned briefly in Chapter 4. In contrast to the "special groups," many of which tend to be merely letterhead organizations with a small working nucleus, the clubs are real social units. Like the special groups, the clubs may operate under or separate from regular auspices.

In his pamphlet, *Practical Politics,* prepared some years ago for the New York Republican County Committee, Daniel J. Riesner has given a good, brief outline of the operations of the more traditional, party-affiliated club.

The District Club

The district club is practically a semi-social political organization. It is organized under the supervision of the district leader. Generally, men and women active in the political organization and the county committee are also active in the club, but this is not always the case.

The main purpose of the club is to attract people who want to be close to the political scene, to know the leader, to meet political personalities, and yet who cannot or don't wish to be county committeemen or captains. The club generally holds monthly meetings, and public figures of note attend as speakers. The speaker may, in some rare instance, be the President of the United States, the governor, the mayor, or an important state or city official, a judge, educator, or writer. Speakers at political club meetings generally have real information or matters of interest to impart. In this way club members get to know their way around—what's cooking in town—and in the district—politically. They get to know who is being considered for the nomination for assemblyman or congressman or mayor. They get the chance to vocalize on the subject and very soon become deeply interested.

There isn't a political worker or club member who doesn't consider his opinion as good as the next fellow's, and that's right and good, as it should be. If more people participated in district club activities they would be more aware of the personalities in local politics as well as city and statewide politics.

They wouldn't go to the polls and feel that after voting for governor, President, and mayor they might as well be blindfolded in voting for the rest of the slate. They wouldn't be embarrassed when asked "Who is your congressman, state senator, or assemblyman?" They would know these men personally. They would be less reluctant to write to people they know on public questions that are before our national or state legislatures.

Before they realized what was happening, they would be in politics up to their necks in a painless way and an enjoyable one.

There are other activities at the political club—dances, card parties, district welfare meetings, etc., and it all fits into the political picture firmly, smoothly, and effectively. Before long, the man or woman who joined the political club to see what it was all about, has become a captain and a county committeeman, and from that time on the opportunity for party and public service is limitless.

Many of the newer political clubs differ, however, from this older variety in that they are less permanent, more informal, and often quite divorced from the regular party organization. For a fascinating, inside story of the political club movement of recent years, as well as for the most complete discussion of club functions and organization, see Stephen A. Mitchell's book, *Elm Street Politics* (Dobbs Ferry, N.Y.) 1959. Mitchell is a former Democratic national chairman who directed one of Adlai Stevenson's campaigns. A more clinical, and critical, analysis of the future of such organizations has recently been made by James Q. Wilson in *The Amateur Democrat* (Chicago), 1962, a study of club politics in three cities—New York, Chicago, and Los Angeles.

A useful, condensed manual on *Political Clubs* is currently available from the U.S. Chamber of Commerce as part of its "Action Course in Practical Politics." Moreover the national headquarters of both major parties have from time to time issued manuals on club operations.

Of course, the perennial problem with all such "special groups" and "auxiliaries" is coordination of their efforts with those of the central party organization and campaign structure. Volunteer groups can easily become embroiled in factionalism and dissipate money and time in ways hardly conducive to the main effort. For this reason the professional party leaders frequently look upon such groups with less than enthusiasm. But they have come to accept the citizen groups as necessary to the full mobilization of political potential.

5. THE TRAINING OF WORKERS

Traditionally, the training of political workers has been accomplished primarily through a kind of apprenticeship process. That is, one begins under the general auspices and guidance of someone more experienced. Despite its lack of systematization, many still prefer this approach.

However, a good deal of thought has recently been given

to new methods for training in political action. In many political organizations training is now much more systematic than it used to be. For example, one of the county leader's jobs, as prescribed in the *Democratic County Handbook* is to "hold training sessions."

Of course, the prospective political worker can do a great deal on his own—through observation, conversation, reading, and taking high school and college courses. Or he may join one of the many types of political clubs for young people, women, union members, or businessmen. These organizations are not only recruiting centers but also, directly and indirectly, they are training grounds.

But within the last decade the principal new development in political training has to do with the introduction of systematic short courses often known as *campaign schools*. This kind of one or two day school, which also may be run through a series of five to ten evenings, is especially recommended because of the chance it gives to bring your workers together and kindle and heighten *esprit de corps*. In most local campaigns it is especially important to explain to the workers how they fit into the organization, to discuss the candidates and provide background information on them and the major issues, and to cover the essentials of grass roots precinct work as detailed in Chapter 12.

After such a course there can then be follow-up meetings to deal with special problems, especially through question-and-answer sessions. The National Republican Congressional Committee, for example, has urged in its *Republican Workers' Manual*, "Hold *monthly meetings* [of workers] until October —then *every week* until election day."

For campaigns in larger areas there may be a need for schools about matters above the precinct level. A typical example is the "County Chairmen's Workshop" conducted by the Maine Republican State Committee on September 19, 1964. Some of the subjects of discussion that day were "Teen-Age Republicans—How they can assist us in this campaign," "Citizens for Goldwater," "Publicity," "How to raise funds,"

"How to stage a successful rally," and "How to guard against irregularities." Hundreds—perhaps thousands—of such one- or two-day schools were conducted during the last national campaign, at all political levels.

As for course materials, they can be developed from this book. In addition, the major party organizations usually provide course outlines which will assist in organizing a series of sessions. In addition, a number of private groups have materials available at a price. For example, in 1958 the National Association of Manufacturers began to provide a large manual for a six-session "Political Action Seminar." In early 1959 the U.S. Chamber of Commerce published a series of pamphlets and instructional guides comprising its "Action Course in Practical Politics" which by now has been taken by hundreds of thousands of people.

Still more sophisticated efforts have been undertaken by the Effective Citizens Association of Washington, D.C., a pioneer in political action education for businessmen, the National Center for Education in Politics at New York University, which has been assisting colleges and universities in practical political training, and the American Foundation for Continuing Education in Chicago, which has prepared political materials for adult extension education. The labor unions and the League of Women Voters reach special adult clienteles. Special institutes, such as the Institutes of Practical Politics at Ohio Wesleyan and the Eagleton Institute of Politics at Rutgers, further assist at the collegiate level. Finally, a similar sort of development is just beginning to take hold at the high school level. See, for example, *Practical Political Action: A Guide for Young Citizens* (1962), adapted from the U.S. Chamber of Commerce course mentioned above and published by the Lincoln Filene Center for Citizenship and Public Affairs, Tufts University.

From all of these sources you can obtain suggestions. However, many materials will be too general for particular situations. For example, only you can explain *your* candidates and *your* issues, and determine just what kinds of training are essential for the workers in *your* area. But this is not too difficult, and there are now people in almost all communities of any size who can help you.

6. CONCLUSION

The developments outlined above provide considerable evidence that there has been something of a rennaissance in civic and political education since World War II. The implications of this movement for the political beginner are also important. For the first time in American history, it is now possible for persons contemplating or just starting into politics to obtain relatively easily the training they need. It is also quite clear that the availability of such training has, in turn, stimulated many persons to try their hand at civic and political action, who would not otherwise have done so.

Chapter 7

*Raising
the
Money*

There is no simple solution to fund raising. It is hard work and frustrating at best. But it must be done. Let us, therefore, look at some suggestions about how to do it, particularly those relating to

1. *the magnitude of the task,*
2. *legal problems and restrictions,*
3. *general principles of fund raising,*
4. *special techniques and devices,* and
5. *budgeting and allocation of funds.*

1. HOW MUCH MONEY—WHERE FROM?

No one knows for sure just how much money has regularly been spent in American political campaigning. But careful estimates indicate that the total political costs, including all levels of government, were at least $200 million in 1964, compared to $175 million in 1960, $155 million in 1956, and $140 million in 1952. Viewed another way, this represents an expenditure of close to $1.50 for each potential voter and over $2.00 for each actual voter in the United States.

These are considerable sums, though they do not begin to match the over $2.5 billion wagered annually at race tracks or the more than $5 billion of philanthropic contributions collected yearly. Compared to our annual governmental costs of nearly $1,000 per person, a cost of only a dollar or so per person for elections seems hardly excessive.

A breakdown of political expenditures among governmental levels indicates that, during presidential campaign years, approximately 38 percent of the moneys reported went to district and local campaigning, compared to 48 percent for statewide activities and 14 percent for nationwide efforts. The bulk of these figures have come from our most complete study of campaign finance, *Costs of Democracy* (1960), by political scientist Alexander Heard, chairman of the President's Commission on Campaign Costs in 1961 and now Chancellor of Vanderbilt University.

Using the 38 percent local government figure gives us a sort of base point from which to consider political fund raising as an operational problem. That is, it suggests that any single local campaign by a single party may need up to $.50 for each prospective voter. Interestingly, this rough calculation coincides almost precisely with the most detailed planning estimates now available on the costs of campaigning. These come from the National Municipal League's pamphlet on *The Citizen Association: How to Organize and Run It*.

Money

The bigger the city, the more money a citizen association will need to reach the voters through literature, mailings, advertising and other media of communication. A larger staff will also be required to keep watch over a large and complex government.

This table suggests a minimum scale of budgets for citizen associations in cities of three population brackets:

Population	No. of Cities	Total Budget	Per Capita Budget
25,000 to 150,000	417	$12,500 to $27,000	50c to 18c
150,000 to 500,000	46	$27,000 to $60,000	18c to 12c
500,000 and up	18	$60,000 and up	12c to 3c

Much larger sums could of course be well spent, if they can be raised.

The suggested budgets are only slightly higher than the actual budgets of 11 representative citizen associations in 1953. The budgets ranged from $10,000 to $56,875, with a median of $23,445. Expenditures per capita were as low as 1 1/2 cents and as high as 19 cents. The median was 7 cents.

Those were normal budgets. Organizations that sponsor a slate of candidates may double or treble their expenditures in election years.

Although two associations said they had enough money for an adequate program, the other nine needed an average increase of 38 percent.

Of course, these figures are for the early fifties, and prices have risen. Moreover, many candidates must fight—and pay—their way not only through election campaigns but also through caucuses and primaries. For realistic estimates for your own area you must consult someone who is familiar with the typical costs of campaigning in it.

What are the prospects of raising the kinds of sums mentioned above? Of course, money never comes easily. Nevertheless, we know that the proportion of the population contributing to campaigns has been increasing. According to data from the Survey Research Center at the University of Michigan, about 10 million persons contributed something of value to a political campaign in 1960 compared to 8 million in 1956 and 3 million in 1952. All told, probably 10 percent of American adults have made political contributions of one sort or another in recent years.

As to our giving potential, a series of polls by George Gallup, taken between 1943 and 1960, suggest that from one-fifth to one-third of the voters "might" give $5 to the party of their choice if asked to. This has indicated a small gift potential of up to $100 million.

As an experiment, the American Heritage Foundation in cooperation with the Advertising Council and the national committees of both major parties made the first really all-out effort to attract small contributions in large volume in the 1958 campaign. The Foundation has reported that its "Don't Pass the Buck—Give a Buck" campaign brought in "about $5 million of new money from small donors to both the Republican and Democratic parties." The Republican National Committee made $2 million from a one-month drive, while the Democratic Committee got more than $750,000 from a four-day doorbell-ringing campaign. The rest came in through simultaneous state and local efforts.

After 1960 Senator Goldwater was especially successful in attracting small contributions. Herbert E. Alexander, head of the research staff of the recent President's Commission on Campaign Costs and now Executive Director of the Citizens' Research Foundation, which is engaged in the on-going study of campaign costs and finance, has stated that Goldwater received $5,500,000 from some 300,000 contributors between 1962 and the time he won the Republican presidential nomination.

This kind of evidence has caused both parties in recent years to move much more in the direction of drives for small sums from a wide base of contributors than ever before. But, despite these efforts, they are not enough. Larger gifts must be sought too. Every legitimate source must be tapped. The limitations are only in your imagination, energy, and organization.

2. LEGAL CONSIDERATIONS

It is not possible here to go into detail concerning all of the legal problems and technicalities involved in political fund raising. But you should know that there are both federal and state statutes governing these matters in nearly all areas. It is also essential that anyone running a political organization, club, or committee *consult a lawyer* or law committee before soliciting funds. This is a must. For a good summary of most of the statutes you can consult *Regulation of Campaign Finance*, a pamphlet by Pamela Ford, published by the Bureau of Public Administration of the University of California at Berkeley.

The broad guidelines which everyone in politics ought to know about have been summarized in a *Fund-Raising Manual* by the Republican National Finance Committee.

Legal Considerations

Special laws place some limitations on the solicitation of political contributions.

Contributors are well advised to obtain advice from their own legal counsel on matters on which they are in doubt.

The following rules summarize briefly some legal aspects on which all persons soliciting political contributions ought to be informed:

1. Corporation checks are not acceptable. Corporations cannot make political contributions. There is no exception.

2. Unincorporated companies, partnerships and individuals can contribute.

3. All contributions must be accompanied by a name; no anonymous gifts can be accepted.

4. An individual's contribution of more than $3,000 to any one committee is subject to gift tax. (See below.)

5. Contributions are *not* deductible for income tax purposes.

The following restrictions on political fund raising are established by Federal statutes:

It is *not lawful* for one federal official or employee to solicit or receive campaign funds from another federal employee or official. Political solicitation by anyone in any federal building is unlawful. . . .

It is *lawful* for any official or employee to make a voluntary contribution to any political party that he may prefer. An employee cannot be forced to make a contribution, and must not be discriminated against for not doing so.

It is *unlawful* for any national bank, or any corporation, or any labor organization, to make a contribution or expenditure in connection with any election to any political office, or in connection with any primary election or political convention or caucus held to select candidates for such office.

The (Federal) Hatch Act prohibits any person from making contributions in an amount in excess of $5,000 during any calendar year, or in connection with any campaign for nomination or election, to or on behalf of any candidate for election to federal office, or to or on behalf of any committee or other organization engaged in furthering, advancing, or advocating the nomination or election of any candidate for any such office or for the success of any national political party. This section, however, does not apply to contributions made to or by a state or local committee, or other state or local organizations. The act also provides that no political committee shall accept contributions aggregating more than $3,000,000, or make expenditures aggregating more than $3,000,000 during any calendar year.

Contributions of over $3,000 to any one committee are subject to gift tax. Under the current community property tax law, a husband and wife can each give $3,000 to a committee without being subject to gift tax.

Until 1962 it was also unlawful for corporations to purchase goods or advertising, the proceeds of which benefited any candidate for office. Moreover, the expenditure of corporate funds for even the nonpartisan promotion of employee political activity was also in doubt at this time. However, as a result of a recommendation by the President's Commission on Campaign Costs in early 1962, the Internal Revenue Service issued Ruling 62–156 in September, 1962. This ruling specified that certain expenditures for politically impartial purposes could be treated as deductible for income tax purposes. These expenditures are: (1) advertising to encourage the public to register, vote and contribute to the party of their choice; (2) costs of encouraging employees to do the same; and (3) costs of sponsoring politically impartial debates between candidates. A still more recent federal court decision suggests that there are really few limits to the purchase of advertising space in even partisan political publications.

These developments in loosening federal restrictions on corporate political expenditures to some extent counterbalance a series of court decisions in the 1950s, which similarly loosened restrictions on labor unions,

Nevertheless, the use of money in politics is still governed by a considerable network of state and local as well as federal statutes. Again, consult with and follow the advice of your legal adviser or law committee. This is no realm for the amateur.

3. MONEY MANAGEMENT

Here we will be concerned with the organization for and administration of political fund-raising campaigns. The most systematic efforts in this direction have been made by the Republican Party. For a number of years the Republicans have worked on what is termed the "united fund-raising plan." This involves a coordinated effort among national, state, and local levels resembling, though on a national scale, the type of drive associated with local Community Chests. Generally speaking, the moneys collected by these drives are divided according to agreed-on ratios among the party organizations at the various levels.

The basic fund raising unit is the state finance committee, associated with the state party organization. This committee has a state finance chairman who directs the efforts of three or so regional directors. Operating under the general supervision of the regional directors, but with considerable freedom, are the county units. Figure 4 comes from a *Fund-rais-*

ORGANIZATION OF A TYPICAL COUNTY DIVISION OF THE OHIO REPUBLICAN FINANCE COMMITTEE

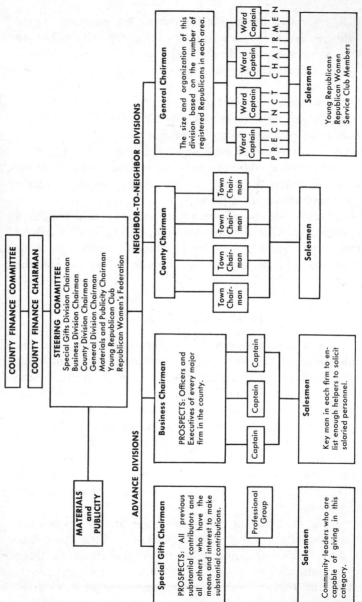

Figure 4

ing Manual of the Ohio Republican Finance Committee. The "Advance Divisions" shown on the chart concern themselves with solicitations for the larger contributions, while the "Neighbor-to-Neighbor Divisions" represent door-to-door solicitations of smaller amounts. By no means have all counties, in Ohio or elsewhere, undertaken the solicitation of small gifts during each campaign; and sometimes mail order solicitation has replaced the door-to-door canvassing. But equivalents of the "Advance Divisions" are almost always operative. In addition, some cities as well as many individual candidates will have supplementary fund raising organizations of varying degrees of complexity.

As to the mechanics of fund raising, detailed guides are available from both national committees and most state ones as well. However, a good, brief summary of basics is contained in the following excerpt from the *Manual of Practical Political Action* of the National Citizens Political Action Committee.

Finance

. . . While there must be a sense of reality in conceiving a program, nothing less than an effective program should be accepted as the minimum for which funds are sought. It costs less money to set sights high. A feasible program requiring considerable expenditures will attract money. A skimpy program, obviously insufficient to accomplish the announced objectives, will seldom attract enough funds for its execution. . . .

You're Asking For It

The fund-raising activities of an organization will be simplified by strict adherence to the following rules:

1. Fund raising must not be separated from the work of the organization.

2. The program of the organization must have genuine appeal, must strike home, and it must give some real promise of success.

3. Fund raising activities must promote the actual program of the organization.

4. Evidence of good management—good budgeting and bookkeeping procedures—should be shown to gain the confidence of those who give and will give financial support. . . .

Money With Meaning

Activities designed primarily for revenue must promote the actual program of the organization. Just as people don't organize for the sake of organizing, they don't give money for the sake of giving. Every fund raising activity should have its political significance, exclusive of the fund raising aspect. For example: A dinner isn't held to raise funds. It is held to push a particular issue or issues and the funds are raised to carry the fight still further.

And it is particularly important that political organizations employ good managerial and bookkeeping methods, not only to comply with legal requirements, but to establish the feeling of confidence on the part of members and contributors.

Fund raising activities require an able staff person or volunteer administrator with a sense of programing. In many communities excellent volunteer or professional personnel can be recruited from the leading charitable organizations. Professional fund raisers know how to organize and carry through campaigns, and they are experienced in breaking down the inhibitions of volunteers who don't like to ask for money.

If plans are made to use professional fund raisers, references should be closely checked and only persons completely sympathetic to the organization's objectives should be considered. Fund raisers should not be hired on a percentage basis. They should be part and parcel of the organization, either as volunteers or paid workers.

Sources of Funds

Almost all of the countless methods of raising funds for organizations can be classified under the following major headings:

1. Dues—annual or monthly payments by members
2. Personal solicitation—individual contacts

3. Group solicitation—meetings, rallies, etc.
4. Direct mail—appeal letters
5. Sales—stamps, buttons, etc., for profit

Dues

It is rare that a political organization can meet all the costs of an effective program through a system of membership dues. The great majority of members can pay only minimum dues and the mere servicing of the members themselves with literature, meeting announcements, etc., generally eats up all dues moneys without providing the other funds needed to carry programs forward.

Dues are important, however, in order to build organization loyalty and provide the great sense of participation that comes from helping to pay the way.

A common, and not generally satisfactory, practice of some organizations is to use systems of graduated memberships: regular, sustaining, contributing, sponsoring, etc., with each at a different rate. While the memberships do not carry different privileges, the system appears undemocratic. In only a few cases does it have merit; in most it serves as a restriction on contributions. One-hundred-dollar sponsorship categories, for example, raise psychological limits for people able to give many times that amount.

Dues should be established at a figure that will cover all the basic organizational needs; in other words, the basic budget should be prorated among the entire membership. This is obviously not feasible with new, small organizations, where the immediate needs are greater than the membership can possibly cover. But in well-established organizations dues should bear some relationship to the basic budget.

If the organization is large and well-established with a working ward and precinct organization, it is possible to arrange systems of monthly dues with a minimum of bookkeeping difficulties and a greater yield than from annual dues. As a general rule, however, it is probably best to arrange for minimal annual dues and use the organization machinery for special assessments, when the membership recognizes the need and approves the collection.

Personal Solicitation

There are distinct advantages to the personal solicitation system of collecting funds, if it is properly carried out. Personal contact by a capable volunteer solicitor, well versed in the facts, knowing the needs of the organization, its accomplishments and its projected program, will produce more dollars per person than any other method.

Yet personal solicitation often fails from lack of organization and bad assignment of solicitors. A personal solicitation drive should be well organized, and as with all fund raising the backbone of the operation is the compilation of the prospect lists.

Once compiled, the lists should be broken down by characteristics of its component parts, i.e., businessmen, club women, doctors, etc. The corps of carefully trained solicitors should then be asked to scrutinize the lists with an eye to selecting those they know or feel they can contact with greatest ease. Individual solicitation cards with the pertinent information about the person to be contacted should be given the solicitor when he volunteers to accept a particular assignment. The soliciting group should discuss the remaining names to determine who in their number should take each name or where the proper solicitor for the particular prospect can be found. Social, business, and professional factors should be considered in discussing each major prospect in relation to the available solicitors.

The foregoing comments have particular validity in the pursuit of sizable contributions. Smaller gifts and door-to-door personal solicitations require an equal amount of careful planning, but with less emphasis on the personalities of solicitor and prospect and greater emphasis on solid coverage of the area.

Group Solicitation

The principal advantage of group solicitation is a highly important psychological factor: the desire of the individual to participate and have his participation known. While there are many people who prefer anonymity, there is an even larger group who prefers to give open and public testimony to their beliefs. They like to stand up, announce a gift, and be counted among the active participants in the movement. . . .

Group solicitations take a number of different forms, from huge mass meetings to small gatherings of a dozen or so people in a private residence or hotel meeting room.

Direct Mail

Successful direct-mail fund appeals require expert preparation to produce results justifying the expenditures and the time-and-energy-consuming operations involved.

Direct-mail appeals require (1) good lists, (2) proper signatures for the appeal letter, (3) adequate presentation of all essential information, and (4) material which will win immediate attention and action on first reading.

The use of mail appeals should be well timed to coincide with wide-spread publicity of the organization's activities. The name of the organization and the signer of its appeal must inspire confidence. In a personal, face-to-face solicitation, the personality of the solicitor and the information he presents can inspire such confidence. It is more difficult to put personality on paper and anticipate the mood of the recipient at the time the mailing piece arrives.

Show them Results

"Single-time givers" are more often the product of poor organization management than the result of the contributor losing interest in the issue or organization or candidate which first inspired him to give. Contributors expect to see results for their money, and it is important to keep them informed of the uses to which their contributions are put.

Even prior to the issuance of reports, the well-managed organization will make certain that each contribution is promptly and warmly acknowledged and that all services (literature, etc.), which have been promised the contributor reach him promptly.

The successful organization will have few single-time

givers; it will show a record of ever-increasing contributions from the same people.

4. SPECIAL TECHNIQUES

More and more the parties are emphasizing a variation of what in other circles has for some time been termed "annual giving." That is, they are encouraging regular contributions from party supporters. This kind of giving assists greatly during the leaner off months and years. It also helps provide funds early in a campaign, at a time when they can be best budgeted for expenditure. Too often, party campaign funds come in at the last moment and too late for best utilization.

PLEDGE CARD—1965 SUSTAINING MEMBER
of the PENNSYLVANIA DEMOCRATIC STATE COMMITTEE

I wish to become a Sustaining Member under the following category:

☐ 25 cents monthly
☐ 50 cents monthly (includes free year's subscription to *Pennsylvania Democratic News*)
☐ One Dollar monthly (includes free year's subscription to *Pennsylvania Democratic News*)
☐ Five Dollars monthly (includes free year's subscription to *The Democrat* and *Pennsylvania Democratic News*)

☐ Ten Dollars monthly (includes one complimentary ticket to Democratic State Committee's 1965 Fund-Raising Event and free year's subscription to *Pennsylvania Democratic News*)
☐ Twenty Dollars monthly (includes two complimentary tickets to the 1965 Fund-Raising Event and free year's subscription to *Pennsylvania Democratic News*)

Note: ☐ Initial payment enclosed. ☐ Bill me on a quarterly basis.
　　　☐ Althought I cannot complete Pledge Card, I wish to contribute _____ (enclosed) to help support the Democratic State Committee in 1965. Checks payable to Pennsylvania Democratic State Committee.

NAME _____COUNTY _____
　　　　　　　　　(please print)

ADDRESS _____
　　　　　　　　　(street)　　　　　　　　　　　　　　　　(city)
PENNSYLVANIA DEMOCRATIC STATE COMMITTEE, 510 N. THIRD ST., HARRISBURG

Figure 5

First, a typical solicitation card is shown just above. The card also shows the benefits attached to each level of giving. However, very few party organizations at any level have as yet been able to survive on sustained annual giving of this type. The reason is partly that this kind of solicitation is new in politics, but also because it requires good lists of prospects and constant attention. These requisites many party organizations, especially at the local level, are ill-equipped to provide.

Nevertheless this kind of personal solicitation effort, either by mail or door-to-door is gradually becoming more common and more effective. The Minnesota Republican organization, for example, has been especially successful in its Neighbor-to-Neighbor campaigns. On a smaller scale the Democrats have been reported as equally successful in Montgomery County, Maryland.

Then, there are the fund-raising efforts typified by the Lincoln and Jefferson Day dinners of the two major parties. Many state and local organizations have used them too, as indicated in the Merriam example in Chapter 3. In 1960 through two evenings of nationwide dinners involving closed-circuit television—one a "Dinner with Ike" and the other a "Campaign Dinner"—the Republicans grossed about $7,700,-000. The Democrats have been equally active in utilizing the fund-raising dinner. Between January 1, 1961, and June 7, 1963, President Kennedy attended over twenty such affairs which, all told, grossed the Democratic Party almost $10,000,-000. Both parties provide guides for running this kind of affair.

Still more recent (in their present form) are the "almanacs," "buying-guides," and "yearbooks" put out by, especially, the Republican state organizations. The *Pennsylvania Almanac and Buyers' Guide* (5th edition, 1964), published by the Republican State Committee, would appear to have grossed the Committee as much as $200,000, based on advertising rates of at least $1,000 a page. In the same year the Democratic National Committee grossed several times that sum from the sale of advertising in its national convention program. Some local organizations—for example, the Tompkins County Republican Committee of New York—have also utilized this type of publication as a means for legally attracting advertising revenues and bolstering party income.

Finally, there are myriad miscellaneous ways to raise money for political purposes. Many of these—such as silver teas, subscription bridge games, fashion shows, bazaars, and cake sales —are peculiar to women's groups for obvious reasons. A good summary list is contained in the following item put out by the Office of Women's Activities of the Democratic National Committee.

Money-Makers Galore!

Here is a round-up of fund-raising ideas. These are in addition to the traditional nationwide projects all Democrats take part in: Sustaining Membership Program—Democratic Party Night—Dollars for Democrats Drive and Democratic Woman's Day, both in the Fall. Jefferson-Jackson Day Dinners are regular money raisers, too!

The suggestions below will help fill the till the year round. Make your projects so intriguing *everyone in town will want to come!*

WOMEN'S EXCHANGE

Most profitable of all permanent projects is a well-located sales outlet for crafts, second-hand goods, home-baked products.

Added Attractions. A rental service on pictures, baby equipment, party equipment (punch bowl), major household tools (floor waxer). Include used paperback books, sewing patterns, children's books and costumes. (Put a playpen in the corner for toddlers so that mothers may browse.)

Services. Serve as a message center and source of civic information.

AUCTIONS

A regular bimonthly auction with attractive articles can build a reputation, attract a growing clientele. Give it a name ("Country," "Attic & Trunk"). Sell refreshments. Train your own auctioneers.

VARIATIONS

Chinese Auction. Everyone who bids on an article must pay the amount he raises the preceding bid even though he is not the successful bidder. The article goes to the highest bidder who pays the full bid. A kitchen timer may be used to cut off the bidding.

Silent Auction. May be held during any meeting. Bidders place written bids in receptacle provided near articles on display.

"Hired Hands" Auction. Everyone donates an hour or two of work (to clean basement, mow lawn, iron, mend, type). Services are auctioned off.

SCHOOL DAYS

People will pay for self-improvement! Charge a fee for:
Lectures on child psychology, money management, travel.
Courses in painting, modern dance, home nursing, knitting, hat-making, public speaking, ceramics.
Charm school, slimnastics classes; garden clinic.

TOURS AND TEA

You may charge for refreshments plus the work of organizing—even for tours of public institutions. Take people to see:
Historic Sites. (If your group is the first to plot the historic tour, put up permanent signs at points of interest as a community project—if possible, "Courtesy of the Democratic Party of ———.")
Modern and traditional homes.
Kitchens, gardens, basement workshops; state capitol.
Factories.

BAZAARS AND FAIRS

Have a theme ("Pioneer Days," "South American") with appropriate costumes, posters, foods, music, short movies. Try a "Wedding Anniversary Fair" (booths with traditional classes of goods—1st Anniversary Booth with paper products, 10th with tin, etc.).

Expand sales with remnants, "dress-ups" for girls, men's tie exchange. Ask for and add to your stock the unclaimed articles which accumulate in public places like hotels, bus stations, and at the dry cleaner's and shoe repairer's. Take large-lot consignments from stores of articles they want to "move."

Add variety with demonstrations (sewing machine,

beauty products, potter's wheel), tea-leaf readings, hand-writing analysis, puppets, magician. Have equipment on hand to cut records of voices. Get an artist to do quick caricatures or cut silhouettes.

Drum up trade on the spot with a circus barker, roving "sandwich man," portable public address system.

SHOWS

At some of these, *you can* not only *charge admission* but *sell items* displayed, too!

Paintings, prints, sculpture.

Handicrafts, hobbies.

Local History Show. Include photos; maps; deeds; old books; old farm, business and household equipment.

Family portraits and heirlooms.

Collections. Stamps, coins, guns, campaign souvenirs, souvenir spoons.

Camera Fans' Show. Give prizes for best shots in various categories: nature, still life, sports, children.

Fashions. Try a "Wedding Gown Review." Show wedding pictures, presents, invitations. Have a commentary on styles and history of the times.

Skits and dramatics. Send for entertaining Democratic skits.

HOME TOWN SERVICES

Souvenir Plates. If your town (or state) has not yet developed a souvenir plate, negotiate with a china manufacturer to have one designed and made. Handle the promotion and sales.

Town or Democratic Cookbook. Publish the favorite recipes of local women. Add those of some of the good men cooks!

Town History. If no one has yet written a pamphlet history of your town, have one of your talented members do so. Print and sell it.

PARTIES

New and old. Square dance, lawn party, pool splash party, concert (jazz or classical), theater or movie party (get a low group rate and add to ticket price for your profit), turkey or skeet shoot, moonlight cruise, hay or sleigh ride.

Dinners, teas, picnics. Make your dinner progressive, gourmet, international, food freezer. Make your tea silver, green (folding money), musical, book review. Try a barbecue, clam bake, weiner or corn roast.

OLD RELIABLES

Celebrities. People will always buy tickets to "see stars." *Novelties.* Donkey-decorated items are stand-bys. Send for "Fund Raising with Novelties."

5. CONTROLLING THE OUTGO

There is little published information about how to budget and plan political expenditures. This stems in part from the uncertainties of both income and probable campaign requirements. Certainly, political financial planning is difficult. But it is not impossible and it must be done or the coffers will be dry much before election day.

As part of its "united" fund-raising plan, the Republican Party recommends that state and county fund-raising organizations have a separate budget committee to go over the spending plans of local organizations and candidates in some detail in order to see that the ultimate allocations are likely to be used to advantage. Prospective donors also appreciate evidence that their money will be wisely spent. It is likely that the use of this sort of separate financial "controller" will increase.

Of course, budgeting requires some idea of costs. In the course of a recent civic affairs campaign among its employees, the Pittsburgh Plate Glass Company published the following "list of essentials" for a campaign in an average large city, together with average prices:

Large billboard	$120 (per month rental)
Junior-size billboard	$17 (per month rental)
30-second spot commercial on radio	$15

1-minute radio commercial	$32
1-minute TV time (local coverage)	$100
½-hour closed circuit TV in a state or urban area	$10,000 (maximum)

Political posters:

11 x 17 inches, one color	$28 (per 100)
11 x 17, two colors	$36 (per 100)

Mass mailing (printed letter message) $62 (per 1,000)

Newspaper advertisement—ranges from 75¢ per column inch to over $3,000 per page depending upon circulation.

Hand card of candidates—two colors $16 (per 1,000)

Meeting halls   Varies, usually 50¢ per person

In addition, one will want to keep in mind such additional expenses as rent for a campaign headquarters and the cost of speakers' fees and travel allowances, sound trucks, postage for mailings, telegrams, campaign newspapers, campaign buttons, book matches with your candidate's name and picture, and other special gimmicks.

Information is also scarce concerning typical allocations of funds among particular budget items, especially for local campaigns. However, the available data suggest that, while national campaigns utilize a high proportion of radio and television time, local campaigns can most effectively emphasize precinct work together with literature preparation and distribution. This is indeed the import of the few budgets that have been suggested.

In his *How to Run for Office* (1960) James Ertel says to plan at the local level on 10 cents per voter, exclusive of radio and TV expenses. He then recommends the following budgetary guidelines: "A general breakdown of expenditures is to allow 25 percent for professional services (in most cases a public relations man), 15 percent for printing, 20 percent for postage, and 40 percent for advertising and headquarters expenses." He feels this allocation will not only provide adequate general publicity but also provide sufficient "working tools" for your precinct workers in direct personal contact with the voters.

One finds a similar emphasis in *How to Get Into Politics* by Oliver Carlson and Aldrich Blake. Here the authors suggest a "prunable" budget, on the assumption that most candidates will be unable to raise the funds they originally plan on obtaining. Beginning with the most essential items and ending with the least important, the following very rough budget can be interpolated from the authors' discussion: miscellaneous and reserve fund, 10 percent; precinct work, 20 percent; literature preparation and distribution, 10 percent; advertising, billboards, and publicity, 35 percent; headquarters and paid staff, 20 percent; and radio, 5 percent.

Alexander Heard's studies of actual proportionate expenditures in local campaigns generally confirm budgets along the above lines. However, in his pamphlet *Money and Politics*, Heard also notes the useful information that most local political organizations reserve about 22 percent of their funds for election day activities.

Nevertheless, what is considered for one budget as compared to another will depend on local conditions, and especially the activities of your competition.

6. CONCLUSION

Here one can only stress again that money is essential in politics. However, the following advice which Raymond Moley offers in his pamphlet, *The Political Responsibility of Businessmen*, is also most appropriate.

Avoid Lavish Spending

Money is necessary, but it can hurt as well as help. Waste is an institutional habit of political organizations. The vital component in any organization is the unpaid energy of devoted workers. Inevitably, demagogic opposition is going to attack the people who create a prodigal auxiliary as "fat cats," "minions of wealth," "rapacious big business." Ostentation has killed many a candidacy. British constituency agents operate and get results on a budget that would be incredible in the United States. Labor agents in Britain are not political spendthrifts because they don't have much, and trade unionists watch such things because it is their own money. Conservative agents operate on slim budgets, in part because the law strictly limits them, but largely because they are smart.

Watch the Dollars with Minute Care

Workers' necessary expenses should be paid at fixed times to all alike, and each should know that there are no favored recipients. Jealousy among workers and paid employees can wreck the morale of an organization. Strict accounting should be continuous, not only because compliance with law is required but because the auxiliary should be ready at all times to reveal its finances publicly in the event of attack by the opposition.

Chapter 8

Digging Out the Facts

In our complicated world, issues, ideas, legislation, platforms, and the like often pose difficult problems. Put them all together into a campaign and you have something which may take a great deal of study and thought. Political action demands publicity, speeches, and arguments. These, in turn, require a great mass of data of all kinds.

The point to all this is—good campaigns are dependent on good ideas. And good ideas do not come out of the blue. Therefore, there has been a growing tendency to recognize the importance of research to the political process. Indeed, the rapidly increasing utilization of social science techniques to help determine political strategy and action is one of the most important of the recent trends in American politics.

One result of all this has been the addition of a research

committee and chairman—sometimes referred to as the facts and figures chairman, or the statistical and information chairman—to the usual array of campaign committees. What does such a committee do?

Basically, there are five possibilities. Let us consider each under the following headings:

1. , analysis of general *American voting patterns,*
2. analysis of *local election statistics,*
3. the *social analysis* underlying these statistics,
4. *position and issue research,* and
5. *surveys and polls.*

1. AMERICAN VOTING PATTERNS

Anyone hoping to make a go of politics, even in a small way, must at least be aware of some of the elementary voting habits of the public in this country. It is impossible here to discuss all the voting tendencies now current in this country, even if anybody knew them all. But it is possible to discuss briefly (1) what groups of people always tend to vote a certain way, and (2) what groups of people tend not to vote at all.

The principal factors involved in whether or not people tend regularly to vote a certain way are apt to be such things as family tradition, race, religion, nationality, occupation, income, and military record. When large numbers of people with similar backgrounds are found in the same voting area, then one may expect a large block of votes regularly to be cast in one direction. It is absolutely essential to recognize this fact and direct one's political efforts accordingly.

Much more perplexing is how to analyze your voting district according to who is voting and who is not. Put in the form of a question, this problem becomes: *What kinds of people are most active politically and which are least active politically?*

We know this much for sure: that seldom do more than

90 percent of those eligible to vote actually vote. In states and areas in which one party is habitually the victor, this percentage may decrease until it reaches a low of 10 to 20 percent in some Southern areas.

Some other tendencies of the voting public have been more or less suspected or understood for some time. But, until recent years, there has been very little carefully analyzed data on the kinds of people who stay away from compared to the kinds of people who go to the polls.

One of the most useful studies from the standpoint of a person interested in a general conception of American voting behavior has come from an investigation undertaken by Elmo Roper, one of our best known polling experts. Based upon a sample of 8,000 people over twenty-one years of age and from all types of living conditions, Roper's research demonstrated that there is a consistent tendency for certain population groups to vote and take part in political activity, and for others to stay away from the polls and show little interest in political action. Here are the basic findings in the form of two tables taken from "Political Activity of American Citizens," an article by Roper and Julian L. Woodward in the December, 1950, issue of the *American Political Science Review*. More recent research has only confirmed these general proportions. Our voting habits do not lightly change. It will pay you to study these tables carefully.

In essence, Tables 2 and 3 tell us that anyone interested in getting out the vote is going to have to work harder if he wants large numbers of these kinds of voters to turn out at the polls: (1) women, particularly housewives, (2) young people, especially those under thirty, (3) persons who never got beyond grade school, and (4) those in the lower income brackets.

This means, in turn, that Democratic political workers—who look for many of their votes from among these groups —are probably going to have to work harder to bring out a large percentage of their potential vote than will Republican workers. Fortunately for the Democrats, as the second table shows, there are probably more potential Democratic than Republican voters. So the race may run fairly even, despite the differing tendencies toward political activity of prospective Democrats and prospective Republicans.

TABLE 2. **Amount of Political Activity Exibited by Various Subgroups in the Population**

	Percent Within Each Subgroup Who Are Politically			
	Very Active	Fairly Active	Fairly Inactive	Very Inactive
Subgroups				
"A" economic level	36	33	23	8
Executives	34	29	28	9
Professional people	31	32	25	12
Stockholders	28	30	30	12
College educated	24	28	30	18
"B" economic level	24	26	34	16
Republicans	15	21	39	25
Men	13	19	36	32
People 50 years of age and over	12	17	34	37
People 35–49 years	11	19	39	31
"C" economic level	11	19	38	32
White people	11	17	36	36
Farmers	11	14	35	40
Independents in politics	10	21	37	32
Total adult population	10	17	35	38
People with only high-school education	9	17	40	34
Democrats	9	15	37	39
Nonstockholders	8	15	37	40
Women	8	14	33	45
People 21–34 years of age	8	14	32	46
Laboring people	6	14	37	43
Housewives	6	14	34	46
People with only grade-school education	5	11	33	51
Negroes	5	10	25	60
"D" economic level	3	9	31	57

TABLE 3. Political Orientation of People with Different Political Activity Scores

	Total Sample	Political Activity			
		Very Active	Fairly Active	Fairly Inactive	Very Inactive
Percent of Republicans	29	43	37	32	19
Percent of Democrats	44	38	40	46	44
Percent of Independent	16	16	20	18	14
Percent of Other, Don't Know, and No Answer	11	3	3	4	23

Of course, the available research on American voting behavior can tell us much more than this. See, for example, the references in Chapter 14. However, mastery of information like that above is basic to any concept of campaigning.

2. ELECTION ANALYSIS

The next essential research step is to analyze your local election data to see where your party stands. The method for doing this can be described very simply. In the words of the Washington State Democratic Committee in its *County Campaign Notebook:* "In order to find the percentage of Democratic votes in each precinct divide the total vote cast for each precinct into the number of Democratic votes in a typical race."

What this amounts to operationally has probably been most clearly laid out by the late O. Garfield Jones, political scientist at the University of Toledo, who trained his students in the same technique.

Analyzing an Election

Shortly after the election I get a copy of the complete abstract of votes from the Board of Elections and put each student to work to learn just what did happen in that election to various candidates. The first step is to determine the normal party vote so as to compare any one candidate's vote with this.

The normal party vote is obtained by plotting the vote of two or three state candidates who have no special vote pull in Toledo and therefore received just the normal party vote. Sometimes a simple comparison will show that one can take the vote for a single official as typical, when his vote is the median of that for several candidates. This will save considerable time. For example, the median or normal Republican vote in 1950 was for Toledo best indicated by that of lieutenant governor.

Each student must have a 3 x 5 card for each township. On that data card he writes the township vote for lieutenant governor and the township vote for his own candidate. Then he shuffles these cards so that the smallest vote for lieutenant governor is on the first card, the card with the next lowest vote for lieutenant governor is card number two, and so on to the card with the largest vote for lieutenant governor as card number 15 for the last township. Plotted on graph paper, this gives you the nearest to a straight line, smoothest curve, for the normal Republican vote. Then you plot the vote for your own particular candidate, township by township, and run a line through these plotted marks. It becomes obvious where your candidate ran ahead or behind the normal party vote.

When your candidate runs appreciably ahead or behind the normal party vote, you then plot the vote by precincts for that township to see in what specific precincts your candidate did especially well or the reverse. Since most precincts tend to contain identifiable political, social, religious or other groups, you can now make a personal check with political workers, prominent citizens, etc., to find out why your candidate did extra well or poorly in this identifiable group.

It is by this kind of detailed analysis that you learn whether *your candidate did well,* or whether *his opponent did poorly.* It was by this kind of analysis that a student, working for Michael DiSalle in the Bricker—DiSalle campaign for United States Senator in the fall of 1952, learned that DiSalle's gains in the colored precincts because of his work for federal housing were offset by his losses in the Hungarian precincts (normally Democratic) where a federal housing project was being opened to Negroes, contrary to the original agreement for segregation when that Hungarian project was first constructed.

I have done many similar kinds of analyses and cite the above example to show how revealing this precinct curve is for one candidate or one issue when compared with a pertinent normal curve. This technique can even be used to check on the effectiveness of a precinct leader. In 1950 this technique quickly spotted the precinct where the Republican precinct leader fell ill early in September and for several reasons the ward leader was unable to send to a substitute to take his place.

Just one more point as to scientific method. We have found that an outstandingly favorable vote in one precinct may be due to entirely different reasons from that of an equally favorable vote in a distant precinct. What this technique does is to localize the abnormality in a specific precinct, so that it may be studied at first hand, just as the physician, finding that you have a temperature, starts hunting for a sore spot or other abnormality to localize the infection. Having localized the infection his next step is to learn what kind of infection it is, what caused it, and how serious it is. Then he may be able to do something about it.

As you can see, this technique involves no college mathematics. It is merely a graphic device for localizing an abnormal vote trend in a specific precinct so that a first-hand study can be made as to the individual or group influence that caused it.

The above technique provides a diagnostic tool which, though simple, may indicate where action is required. All too seldom is this sort of analysis used. As Jones once wrote, his technique is a "protest against the unscientific basis of so many post-election explanations. Induction should precede deduction, when possible." And it usually is possible if one cares to make the attempt. Nor does it require complicated and difficult procedures.

3. SOCIAL ANALYSIS

Once you "localize the abnormality," as Jones has put it, what next? This means that you must now obtain some conception of the social composition of your district: what sort of people are in it, their standard of living, their occupations, their religious preferences, and so on. Only then can you begin to figure out "why?"

Knowledge of this sort will let you relate your district to general American voting patterns, so that you can anticipate some of your campaign problems. The data will also permit you to pinpoint your campaign strategy where it may do the most good.

The *Manual of Practical Political Action*, issued in the late forties by the National Citizens Political Action Committee, contains one of the earliest—but best—discussions of what is involved in this kind of research. "As a minimum," the NCPAC says, "no committee should consider itself seriously engaged in political activity unless it can provide answers to the following questions."

These are the questions, somewhat paraphrased because a few of them are out of date in their original form:

1. What is the total number of adult citizens in your district?

2. Do you have the population figure broken down by ward and precinct?

3. What was the total Republican and Democratic vote in previous elections?

4. What estimates can be made of the independent vote in previous elections?

5. What is the total foreign-born population of your district? What is its nationality breakdown?

6. What is the potential Negro vote in your district? How have the Negroes who live in your district voted in the past?

7. What AFL-CIO union locals have headquarters in

your district? Independent unions? How many members in each by ward and precinct?

8.   What other organizations are important in the life of the voters of your district? Where are their members located and what are their voting tendencies in previous elections?

9.   How many residents of your district have come of voting age since the last election?

10.   Who are the key civic, religious, educational, labor, foreign-language, professional and Negro figures in your district?

11.   Who are the Democratic and Republican party county, ward, and precinct committeemen? What is their background?

12.   What is the average income in your district? Lowest? Median? How is it distributed geographically?

13.   Do you have a complete block-by-block analysis of your district, showing rent, income, nationality, etc.?

14.   What have been crucial issues in previous campaigns and how did your district react toward them? Which are of paramount interest?

As the NCPAC concludes, "If you don't have the answers to these questions, you haven't begun to know your community."

Now, then, how do you go about getting such information?

Here is the same committee's answer to this question, updated for current convenience. It discusses the details involved in analyzing a congressional district to find out what makes it tick. However, the same methods of analysis can be used in any other kind of political district with equal effect. For instructions on the use of census data, as required in this procedure, see almost any librarian.

How to Analyze a Congressional District
SOURCES OF DISTRICT DATA

Analyzing a congressional district requires certain tools. Sources for the researchers and analysts are many and inexpensive. Every major department of the federal government as well as the major administrative departments of the states and most large cities have available the source material essential for an effective congressional district analysis.

The U.S. Census Bureau of the Department of Commerce and the Department of Labor are especially equipped with the needed information. Besides these government sources, there are a large number of organizations ranging from local chambers of commerce to social service and even church agencies which gather valuable information on industrial and social conditions.

An analysis of your congressional district will be divided into two general sections. The first is research on district voting statistics, and the second, on the human and physical, the economic and social make-up of the district itself.

For convenience, here are the numbered steps for getting the voting statistics in your district:

1. Check the Congressional Directory to find what territory is covered in your congressional district.

2. Write to your secretary of state at your state capital for as detailed a breakdown of the election statistics in the state as he will make available for the public. If these figures are not detailed enough (the amount of detail varies from state to state), you can get the county, city, or town data from the clerks of those units either by writing for them, or if they are not allowed to be sent to the public, by asking permission to copy them in the clerk's office. These statistics should be broken down according to precincts or wards in cities and towns. For the 1966 campaign, it is necessary to learn what happened in the 1964 election, and the 1962 election as well, so that you will know what may occur if a large vote is not turned out in 1966. Check the 1964 campaign for the presidency, and check the voting figures for senator in the states which had a senatorial race, and for representative.

3. Registration figures by party can be obtained from the same sources. Sometimes this information can only be secured from separate boards of registration (state, city, or county—it varies locally).

4. A comparison of steps 2 and 3 will show how large a vote should be recorded as a bare minimum objective.

5. The 1960 Census on Characteristics of the Population will tell you the number of male and female citizens and naturalized citizens over twenty-one—that is, the number of potential voters in each county. There are other tables in the same census that give you the breakdown, often by ward, of the larger cities. These figures can be totaled to make up the congressional district.

If this breakdown is not fine enough, the regional offices of the census have breakdowns by census tract which are available for use in the offices. This goes for all census material.

6. A comparison of steps 2 and 5 will show you how many people could have voted and should vote in the future, but have not yet voted. A fine-comb job of getting them out to register and then to vote will have to be done.

Discovering exactly what kind of congressional district you are working in is the other half of your scientific analysis. Obviously, you must study the various kinds of organizations in your district—political, civic, fraternal, trade union, church, business, and farm. List their leaders, what the leaders and the organizations do, who their membership is, their connections, their policies.

For the broader statistical picture of the entire district, you will find the U.S. Census's various volumes on Housing, Population, Agriculture, and Manufacturing very valuable. They will tell you a great deal about what people do, what kind of homes they live in, what the big industries and crops are, the number of white-collar workers, the age level, the racial composition, numbers of foreign-born people, the most populous towns, the level of education—an almost infinite number of facts.

For an example of what the census volumes contain, glance at the contents for the Housing book: urban and rural areas, rural nonfarm dwelling units, rural-farm dwelling units, metropolitan districts, population per occupied unit, occupancy and tenure, color of occupants, value, and monthly rent, residential structure, type of structure, exterior material, year built, conversion, state of repair, water supply, toilet facilities, bathub or shower, number of rooms, lighting equipment, size of household, persons per room, radio, refrigeration equipment, cooking fuel, heating equipment and fuel, mortgage status, inclusion of furniture in rent, medians.

Careful study of this type of material will give you an overall picture of your district and the interests and needs of the people living in it.

The data thus compiled will enable you to reach many necessary conclusions concerning issues to stress, to whom, where, and how. For you must tailor your campaign to the people in your district and to *their*, not your, preferences, habits, way of life and the like. Only a thorough-going social analysis will give you many of the kinds of information which you need.

4. POSITION AND ISSUE RESEARCH

You might end your research effort at this point if a campaign were not a competitive thing. You must appeal to the voters not only in your own right, but in comparison to anyone running against you. This requires a considerable effort to obtain large quantities of information concerning all those matters which are likely to become issues in the campaign.

Issue research is the most traditional. For generations politicians have been looking up each other's records, so they can capitalize on each other's mistakes. In addition, they must buttress their various positions with the necessary facts and figures. These activities are especially stressed in the current *Democratic Campaign Manual*.

> Political research is one of the most frequently overlooked aspects of a campaign.
>
> The art of political research involves checking into an opponent's record, as far back as he has a record. This means searching newspaper files, the Congressional Record, books, magazine articles, his press releases if they are

available, and any other public statements he may have made.

The research chairman should document the opponent's background as thoroughly as a lawyer prepares a case for court.

The candidate should have full knowledge of his opponent's positions on various issues, any contradictory stands he may have taken, any off-the-cuff statements he may have made that he'd like to forget.

If the opponent has run for office before, a careful check of newspapers in the district for three or four weeks prior to the election should reveal a wealth of material on his positions at that time. The last four or five days before an election may be particularly important, because very often a candidate will make a last-minute pitch for votes through a claim or promise he might not make in a calmer moment.

If the opponent presently holds office, his record will be easier to document. If he is a Republican member of Congress or the Senate, you can receive excellent assistance and cooperation from the Democratic Senatorial or Congressional Campaign Committees. The Democratic National Committee's Public Affairs Division also provides useful information. Previous Democratic candidates who ran aganst the opponent may have records available.

The research director should place someone on the opponent's mailing list during the campaign, so he can obtain the complete text of any statement he issues.

As important as it is, investigating the opponent's record is only one of the research chairman's responsibilities.

He'll probably want to appoint a research committee (or an issues committee) which will study the various issues in the campaign and prepare position and background papers for the candidate on subjects like housing, transportation, civil rights, taxes, foreign policy, and other issues that may be pertinent to the campaign.

These papers should be designed for internal use only; not for publication. They should be frank and factual, and give all sides of any question or issue.

From these position papers, the candidate, probably

through his press secretary, can prepare speeches, statements, and news releases.

The research committee must be prepared to act quickly if the candidate, campaign director, or other key campaign person requires specific, detailed information about an issue, a position, or an individual.

The results of this type of research are often compiled into what has become known as a *fact book*. For example, the *1948 Reference Handbook* of the Republican State Committee of Pennsylvania was the size of a college textbook and contained a vast array of factual materials of possible use to candidates, speech writers, publicity chairmen, and so on.

In 1956, the Republican National Committee had a sizeable *Speakers Book*, while the Republican Congressional Committee published an inch-thick *1956 Speech Kit* which was supplemented in 1958 by a 50-page item, *The Republican Record of Accomplishments by Executive Departments, 1953–57*. The Democrats matched these in 1958 with a concentrated 100-page *Democratic Fact Book*.

In 1964 the Democratic State Central Committee of Michigan published an inch-thick *Legislative Campaign Kit* as part of its effort to defeat Governor George Romney and elect a Democratic state legislature. This compilation was divided into five sections, entitled "Campaign Mechanics," "Campaign Issues," "The Romney Record," "GOP Voting Record, 1963–64," and "Democratic Candidates." The "instructions" on use of the kit, closed with the following: "Your Campaign Kit is not yet complete. From time to time during the Campaign you will receive supplemental materials for the Kit. Special attention will be given to keeping you up-to-date on programs and proposals announced by Congressman Staebler." Staebler was Romney's opponent for governor.

In small areas it will not be feasible to go to such lengths. But even here you can follow the advice given by the Republican National Committee to state, county, and local organizations in the spring of 1965. In its pamphlet, *Where Do We Go From Here*, the Committee urged: "Start intensive research projects on every Democrat office-holder who will be up for re-election in 1965 and 1966. We must have their records in plenty of time to make good use of them in the campaign."

You must know what the opposition is doing and what it is like. And you must have the facts and figures to back up your own point of view.

5. SURVEYS AND POLLS

Most of the research techniques already described have been in use for some time and may be undertaken by a reasonably well-educated amateur. Not so, however, with many of the newer survey and polling techniques, designed to sample, analyze and predict public opinion. These require expert technical knowledge and skill if they are to be really useful. They can also be expensive.

What do polls accomplish that our prior research methods can not? Actually, other research methods are able to do a great deal, but the polls and surveys will do a few key things better and with a great deal more certainty. In their *Plunging into Politics*, Marshall Loeb and William Safire note that surveys and polls can accomplish five important objectives. They can evaluate one candidate's prospects compared to another's. They can regularly measure a party's and candidate's strength. They can portray a party's image and suggest desirable changes. They can advise about the effect of campaign issues and tactics on the public. And, as former Republican National Chairman Leonard Hall wrote in 1960, "They are particularly useful in narrowing issues. At the start of a campaign you may be talking about 15 issues, and then surveys may tell you that people are not interested in 10 of them. So you probe to find out why people seem to be interested in the other five, and you concentrate on those."

Polling is not just asking voters how they are likely to vote. As used today, it is much more sophisticated than this. Murray Chotiner, a main Nixon campaign adviser, stressed this point in a 1955 talk before the Republican state chairmen.

If you have in mind taking a poll for the purpose of determining whether or not your candidate will win, don't waste the money to see whether your candidate is ahead or the other candidate is ahead, because a poll taken six weeks in advance of an election will not tell you how the people will vote election day.

But if you take a poll do it for the purpose of finding out if the people know who is the incumbent—do you know him?—have you heard of him?—what do you think of him?—why do you like him?—or if you dislike him, why do you dislike him?

You then begin to find out the things which you can talk about.

If he happens to be your candidate, you find out why the people are for your candidate, or why they happen to be against him.

. . . a poll . . . helped determine whether Earl Warren would be a candidate for Governor in 1942. We found out that Culbert Olsen, the incumbent Governor, completely outranked Earl Warren as far as being known to the people of California. It was amazing how many people did not know who Earl Warren was, even though he was the Attorney General of California.

Ordinarily, a person might look at that kind of poll and say, "Well, that is a tough one to try and win."

But we found out that there was a large percentage of the people who had heard of Culbert Olsen, who didn't like him, whereas a very small percentage of the people who had ever heard of Earl Warren had anything bad against him. In other words, we took a poll; Earl Warren was not disliked but Culbert Olsen was disliked.

And, by an analysis of the poll, we found out that there were enough people who did not like Culbert Olsen that we could conduct a winning campaign.

At a conference of political scientists in the same year, Malcolm C. Moos of Johns Hopkins University, then chairman of the Republican organization in Baltimore and later a personal assistant to President Eisenhower, outlined several ways in which the Baltimore Republicans had utilized polls. The following is from *The Role of Public Opinion Polls in the Study of Political Parties,* a summary of this conference, published by the Institute of Public Administration at the University of Michigan.

> One of the handicaps the [Baltimore Republican] party faced was the prevalence of straight-ticket voting for the Democratic party. Polling data indicated that among the very sizable Negro population much of this electoral behavior was due to the fact that many members of this group did not know how to vote a split ticket. Having nominated a number of Negro candidates, the party undertook an instructional campaign to encourage normally Democratic Negro voters to split their tickets. . . . This campaign, based as it was on polling data, was in no small measure responsible for the fact that in the face of a sweeping state-wide Democratic victory, the Republicans were able to elect four Negro candidates to the legislature.
>
> The Baltimore Republicans were also able to use polling data as an aid to campaign fundraising. Efforts to solicit contributions for the recent mayorality campaign were hampered because of a general feeling that the Republican candidate had no chance. However, a public opinion poll showed very considerable Republican strength. This fact was emphasized thereafter in fund-raising efforts, with evident success.
>
> Polls can also be used . . . to judge the appropriateness of campaign appeals. In a study conducted in Baltimore during a Democratic primary, it was found that the issues being emphasized by both candidates were quite similar, but were sharply divergent from the set of issues polling indicated to be important in the minds of the voters. The strategy implications for the Republicans were obvious.

Moos also felt that if the regular political leaders utilized polling more often and more effectively, it might help stem the increasing domination of political campaigns by public relations experts. "The resulting relegation of party workers to the status of errand boys," he believed, "has a debilitating effect on the party."

In any event, surveys and polls are being increasingly used

to assist in the design of political tactics and strategy. Many congressmen, senators, governors, and others have found them indispensable. Louis Harris, the well-known pollster who became a personal adviser to the Kennedy brothers, has estimated that the amounts spent for private political polls rose from no more than $75,000 in the 1946 and 1948 campaigns combined to over $1,000,000 for 1956 and 1958. The figure for 1960 alone was probably $1,500,000.

Guidance on the use of professional polling and survey firms is currently available in the *Democratic Campaign Manual* of the National Democratic Committee.

Cost

Survey costs vary greatly, depending upon the size and population of the state, the length and complexity of the survey questions, the urgency of the poll in terms of time, and other variable factors. Minimum fees for a congressional district range from $2,000 to $4,000.

These fees are all-inclusive. They cover the pollster's interviewing expenses, all tabulating fees, preparation of the reports, overhead, and profit. Most polling firms ask 50 percent of the fee when the agreement is made, the remaining 50 percent when the report is ready.

The fees outlined here are for comprehensive surveys. A subsequent reading to update information on the relative standing of the candidates will cost less.

It may be possible to save money by coordinating polling activities through state headquarters, or cooperating with other Democratic candidates to share the expense of a poll or series of polls.

It is unwise to take a poll "just to find out how the candidates stand" or to determine how well the candidates are known. There are certain irreducible minimums in conducting a poll. If money is really tight, a pollster will outline what he can do for what money is available.

Summary

Polls are useful. If a contest is in doubt, and the budget can stand it, a poll should be taken.

The polling firm should be politically oriented, have worked for Democratic candidates before, be able to document its success, and speak the candidate's political language. The Democratic National Committee can provide names of reputable polling firms.

As implied above, it is inadvisable for amateurs to go into survey work on their own. If you have the funds for professional polling, by all means go to one of a number of reputable firms. However, there is one other alternative. If you can find locally, from, say, one of the universities or one of the polling or market research organizations, a person qualified to serve as a professional director or adviser, it is possible for him to train and direct a group of intelligent and well-educated volunteers. Such an approach is much less expensive and can do good work when the supervision is steady and well qualified.

But, again, the essential feature is "the professional."

All this is simply the application of modern research techniques to everyday political work. The use of these techniques will not only give you a far more scientific basis for action but will also save you from some of the more grievous errors of self-delusion.

6. CONCLUSION

Nearly all party organizations, and especially those in closely contested areas, are regularly engaged in most of the types of research outlined above. Research won't supply all the answers, but it can do a tremendous amount to take some of the uncertainty out of what is at best a precarious business.

It is not necessary that you master, personally, all that has been covered here before you start to take an active part in politics. But you should at least commence to look into the various approaches to political research. Sooner or later you will find it absolutely necessary that you understand what research can do when applied to public affairs.

Chapter 9

Planning the Campaign

The ultimate purpose of political organization is to win elections, and this basic fact must always be kept firmly in mind. All party mechanisms are to some extent geared to election campaigning. Therefore, much that is covered in the chapters before and after this one is applicable here.

However, there are some special problems involved in campaigning and it is around these that this chapter has been designed. More specifically, we will emphasize here the following:

1. *the role of the campaign manager,*
2. *campaign management and organization,*
3. *general strategy and tactics,* and
4. *campaign timetables.*

But, first, a word of caution! There is by no means complete agreement on how campaigning ought to be done. Certainly, many local campaigns present special types of difficulties which cannot be dealt with here. Even the more generally oriented materials presented in the following pages contain some differences of opinion and emphasis. Campaigning is still largely an art in which experience plays a major role.

1. THE CAMPAIGN MANAGER

One of the first differences of opinion often arises over the *selection of the campaign manager*. It is generally agreed that a candidate should have something to say about who is to be his campaign manager. Generally speaking, there are two possible choices: (1) the chairman or other leader of a regular party organization, or (2) someone outside the regular party organization.

The tendency these days is toward the latter. However, it is also recognized that all campaign organizations must be closely allied to the regular party organization. Part of the reason for choosing an "outside" person for a candidate's campaign manager lies in the fact that there is often a large number of candidates. Each candidate needs some sort of manager, and it is difficult for, say, a county chairman to give individual attention to the needs of all his different candidates. Therefore, the area chairman is more likely to play a coordinating role for the area party campaign as a whole, with a number of individual campaign managers working closely with him. However, it should be stressed again that this is only a tendency, not a fully general rule as yet.

First, a campaign manager ought to be as experienced as possible. This is seldom a job for the complete amateur. So much depends on experience with local politics and on "whom you know." Occasionally, however, someone with private public relations experience or who has participated in general civic action can make the adjustment and serve exceedingly well. The choice of a manager also depends upon the relationship of the candidate to the party professionals. If he is heading up a reform movement, the candidate may find himself unable to draw upon the usual professional talent. If so, he must look in other directions. In any event, the choice is a crucial one.

The case for a close connection with the formal party organization is fairly obvious, for much of the best professional experience and talent lies within the party structure. The newer trend toward utilization of an experienced volunteer somewhat outside the regular organization has been best put by Murray Chotiner of California in his 1955 talk on "Fundamentals of Campaign Organization" before the Republican National Committee's Campaign School for state chairmen.

> . . . there are many people, whether rightly or wrongly, who still classify themselves as independent voters even though they are registered Republicans, even though they are registered Democrats, and so we always advocate that every candidate for Congress, Governor, Lieutenant-Governor, Senator, or whatever it may be, have his own individual chairman of his campaign committee.
>
> That doesn't mean that the state committee cannot supervise and see that these campaigns are conducted properly. But get a chairman, a prominent citizen recognized for his active participation in the community; someone well known in your district without necessarily having been identified with politics.
>
> Why? Because you are trying to attract to your candidate the votes of the independents and, if you please, of the Democrats as well. . . .

Chotiner's advice to the Republican state chairmen would seem to be most applicable in states like California (his own), where independence runs high and the party organizations are relatively weak. In states and localities where politics is dominated by the party organizations, his suggestions are much less applicable.

For the general role of a campaign manager, the following

discussion, taken from the Republican National Committee's *Campaign Manual* of some years ago, provides a useful guide:

The Campaign Manager

The candidate is the campaign's front man; and the campaign manager is in effect his business manager. He has the overall responsibility of administering its ideas and affairs, and of taking the mechanics of campaign organization and operation off the hands of the candidate. This leaves the candidate free for speeches and top-level thinking on policy and strategy problems. The two must maintain the closest relationship and keep their thinking allied together at all times. In case there should be any disagreement which cannot be worked out through consultation, final decision should be made by the candidate.

The campaign manager's role is not to do the work himself, but to get other people to do it, to make sure that they do it, and to make sure that they do it efficiently. The more he can be assisted with mechanical details, the more effective his role will be. In a large-scale campaign, he should have a full-time, paid secretary, and several assistant campaign managers. He may also wish some additional assistants, preferably women, who can make telephone calls, etc., and speak for him on routine matters. And he will need to rely immeasurably on the headquarters secretary.

With the change on the political scene, the decline of the big-city machines, and the increasing use of volunteers, it is pertinent to point out that in these times campaigns bog down when the little things are not done. They run like clockwork when there are plenty of people to do the little things, for the little things then rapidly mount up into big things. Every precaution should be taken against bogging down with details, errands, and telephone calls.

• • • • • •

The campaign manager, as well as the candidate, should try to avoid staying up late at night, and going through exhausting experiences. The reason for this is that the responsibility for thinking and planning at top level, and for the basic campaign drive, rests on these two people, and those responsibilities cannot be adequately discharged if either one becomes fatigued.

2. CAMPAIGN ADMINISTRATION

For a general discussion of the operations of a party headquarters, most of which is also applicable to a campaign headquarters of any kind, see Chapter 5. This previous chapter also outlines the major types of committees which are likely to be required; and Chapter 13 deals with the special problem of the relatively temporary committees required for election day itself.

Here it is most appropriate to consider the general relationship of the *overall campaign committee* to the rest of the campaign organization. Chotiner's advice below is relevant to either an "insider-directed" or "outsider-directed" campaign.

> . . . of course, you will have a campaign committee.
> Why? Because everyone wants to get in the act.
> If you can imagine a chart with the lines, I would get your committees as far from the campaign manager as possible, because those in campaigns know that you will get as many different ideas on the conduct of the campaign as there are members of committees.
> The manager of the campaign committee serves directly under the candidate and the chairman. After all, it is the campaign manager who has to take advice from any and all of the members of the committees.

There is general agreement as to the lines of campaign authority once a manager has been selected. The following from the Republican National Committee's *Campaign Manual* is especially precise on this matter.

The Need for a clear Campaign Structure
DELEGATION OF AUTHORITY

Many campaigns are run with the loosest and most haphazard campaign structure imaginable, without either clear

lines of authority or clear understandings of responsibility. But such haphazard organization and structure
bring only haphazard results.

The first job of every campaign manager is to set up a
campaign organization with a clear structure. This simply
means, as a practical matter, that every function should be
delegated clearly and specifically to someone, preferably
in writing, with a clear line of authority and a perfectly
clear understanding of responsibility on the part of the
person who is to carry out the particular program. Nothing causes so much trouble as a misunderstanding, and
because of the fluid and dynamic character of a political
campaign, especial care must be taken to prevent misunderstandings in this fast-moving field. And, the need for
clarity increases with the scope of the campaign. . . .

Where possible, the campaign manager should reserve
no administrative or operational responsibilities for himself, but should delegate them all. When a new and workable idea appears on the horizon, he should put somebody
in charge of it as a new program immediately, reserving
for himself the basic role of coordinating, trouble-shoot-
ing, and developing new ideas. He will be busy enough
with those duties.

In addition, he should try to delegate as much of his
administrative and clerical responsibilities, or he will find
himself bogged down in detail, behind in his work, and
with no opportunity to do the thinking at top level which
is the basic job of the campaign manager.

Accordingly, it is best to prepare a campaign organization chart as soon in the campaign as its plan of operation
has been ascertained with reasonable clarity.

The Basic Policy of Decentralization

The foundation of administering the activities of a campaign organization must necessarily be the basic policy of
decentralization. Its prime objective is to bring in new
people continually, to reach constantly further and
further into the ranks of the public for more and more
workers, decentralizing responsibility to an increasing
degree with every new area and project, yet always

maintaining centralized control. Usually, one of the main problems in a political campaign is manpower; more manpower is always needed than can be found, if the campaign is properly organized at the outset and all the potentialities are sounded out.

Decentralization of responsibility can be accomplished in the canvassing division through the appointment of regional captains, precinct captains, and block captains; in the speakers' bureau through the team system and the team captains; similarly in the literature distribution division through the team system and the team captains; and so on. It is important also to remember that people like badges and titles.

Maintaining Centralized Control

Centralized control, in the hands of the campaign manager, who in turn is accountable to the candidate for administration of the campaign, must always be maintained. There are several ways of accomplishing this:

HOLD STAFF MEETINGS

The early stages of every campaign are fluid, subject to constant change and revision, with new people constantly being brought in and new ideas constantly appearing. Thus, in the early stages of a campaign, the campaign manager should hold staff meetings of the chairmen of divisions and other key figures in the organization. These meetings should be conducted on as businesslike a basis as possible. They stimulate ideas, build morale, and provide clear understandings all around.

· · · · · ·

However, staff meetings do not serve a useful purpose once the various divisions have their programs under way, and should then be discontinued.

The chairman of each division may find it useful to call meetings of workers in his division, in order to work out his plans, develop ideas, and recruit new workers.

USE THE TELEPHONE

For political campaigns, the telephone may truly be said to be a wonderful instrument. Volunteers are busy, and they are separated geographically. In a campaign covering a wide area, the factor of distance provides an additional problem. But the telephone is an instrument which can solve both the part-time and the geographical problems. Hence, the campaign manager should keep in touch by telephone, where personal conference is not possible, with all the chairmen of his divisions and the key figures of the campaign. The chairmen of the divisions should be encouraged to acquire the habit of reporting to him, by telephone at least, on the activities of the various divisions, so that the campaign manager may be kept abreast at all times of what is going on. . . .

HOLD MEETINGS OF WORKERS

It is well to have periodical meetings of workers as the campaign runs along, where all of them may mingle and meet with some degree of relaxation. The candidate should be present, and refreshments should be served. If there are to be any speeches, they should be short and to the point. Emphasis should be on relaxation. This enables workers who may not know each other except by telephone, or who otherwise see little of each other, to meet and talk. In the general conversation which will go around the room, everyone will become better apprised of the reasoning and operations of all the divisions in the campaign.

Also, good workers' meetings will build up that wonderful feeling of exhilaration which goes with political work in which people believe, and which they have a chance to do effectively.

Liaison with the Regular Organization

Where the campaign is being put on by an individual club or group, one or more liaison representatives should be officially and clearly designated, whose job it is to keep in touch with the various regular party leaders, to apprise them of developments in the campaign, and to handle any complaints or problems which may arise. Their job it to "keep the regular party leaders happy."

Liaison with the regular organization is also a problem when relatively independent, volunteer groups are supporting a given campaign. Here, Chotiner's recommendations are especially relevant.

> Make sure that you have your campaign geared to reach every single Republican in the territory. Then, of course, make sure that you have a separate organization that is set up of Democrats or independents or whatever you may want to call them.
>
> I think one of the great difficulties and troubles that develop in a campaign . . . is that independent committees, citizens committees, or volunteer committees get the idea that they are above, apart from, and beyond the regular Republican organization. Sometimes the members even look down their noses at the Party. Irrespective of that, it is essential that these committees be organized. They are most effective in winning a campaign. . . .
>
> We [in California] always set up the Democrat committees and citizens' committee and independent committees . . . , but we never let the committee think that it was running the campaign, and we never let them think that they were above and beyond the pale of the regular organization that was going to conduct the campaign.
>
> The reason for it is that your manpower and your womanpower will come from your regular organization. The other groups which you have, whether they be Democrats or independents, will be helpful. They will be the ones issuing the statements for the purpose of appealing to the independents and the Democrats to vote for your candidate, but we learned from experience that they never have sufficient numbers of people to put on a campaign.
>
> In the 1954 election, we found out, I think almost without exception—and I know that there will be many who will disagree with what I am about to say—that the meetings which were not, shall we say, organized as well as they might have been, or the crowds were not as good as they might have been, were those meetings which were held and organized and sponsored under independent committees rather than the regular party organization.
>
> And so may I suggest then that we see to it that the regular campaign organization controls the outside committee. How do we set them up as separate committees?

Obviously we give them separate literature and separate stationery and different color in the printing and separate headquarters and they have their own publicity releases but we always saw to it that no publicity release went out from these organizations unless it was cleared through the parent organization or was not crossing wires.

Following Chotiner's advice above is not always easy, especially if the independent committees are, in fact, fully independent. Nevertheless, if separate organizations of any kind are to be effective, they must suppress factional quarrels and maintain constant liaison with the headquarters which they are supposedly supporting. Chotiner's implication that independent groups often need more and better professional direction is quite correct.

Actually, political professionalism consists of two things: (1) an understanding of how politics and political organizations work, and (2) subordination of nearly everything else to the primary goal of winning an election. Inadequate organizational follow-through and petty squabbles over personalities and issues are the mark of the amateur. He leaves the impression he cares more about himself than about the reason why political organization exists—namely, to win.

3. GENERAL STRATEGY AND TACTICS

One of the first problems any campaigner must tackle is that of his *audience*. To whom should he address himself? The following discussion may assist you in this and related matters. It is from Gus Tyler's discussion of "American Politics: How They Work and How You can Work in Them," in *Guide to Politics, 1954*, prepared by Americans for Democratic Action. Tyler has been chief political adviser to the International Ladies' Garment Workers Union.

To whom is a campaign addressed? Somewhere along in a campaign—or in your life—you will begin to conclude that a campaign is really a ritual, in which the converted speak to the converted and the hustle and bustle of tears and tirade are pure waste.

It may be helpful then to keep perspective on a campaign in terms of its overall purposes:

A campaign is addressed to a variety of groups:

1. The Undecided. These are the people who have no choice in May but will vote in November. In one study, this group was found to be some 28 percent of the electorate.

2. Your Opponent's Fringe. These are the people who are in the opposite camp, but rather unsteadily. You can win over with some real effort.

3. Your Opponent's Supporters. These are the people who will vote for your opponent if they vote, but who will stay away from the polls if, in the course of the campaign, they become uncertain about the intensity of their convictions or because they feel that they are voting for a lost cause and therefore don't want to "throw away a vote."

4. Your Opponent's Workers. These are the backbone of your opponent's organization. They will vote for your opponent but they may not work so hard for him, if their conscience is troubled or if they feel their effort is wasted.

5. Your Own Fringe, Your Own Supporters, and Your Own Workers. These are the opposite numbers of your opponent's and have to be kept in line, pepped up, mobilized against the attempts of your opponent to neutralize them, discourage them, or win them over.

A campaign, then, is not simply directed at the undecided. A campaign is directed at paralyzing your opponent's army and galvanizing your own army: from hard core to outer fringe.

A campaign—viewed in terms of content—contains two major ingredients: the general approach to the public at large and the special approach to given groups within the total electorate.

Normally, a campaign begins with an opening statement that is a broad declaration of policy: the keynote address. The keynote is apt to get the best newspaper play, is apt to have the widest circle of listeners and readers. The great mass of voters who make up their minds early in terms of their basic beliefs, attitudes and prejudices may pay some attention to the keynote address and let the rest of the campaign roll by.

The specific approach to given groups is not simply a way to win over certain elements in a community; it is—in some cases—the only way to break a group or an individual away from traditional moorings and voting habits. A voting group may be conservative and internationalist. If you were a liberal internationalist, you might be able to win this group by emphasizing your internationalism. Groups and individual voters find themselves "conflicted" because of contrary tugs. The wise campaigner puts a little extra pull on the tug that will drag the voter in his direction.

To run an efficient campaign, it is mandatory that you plan. You must coordinate your campaign with the political calendar; you must know to whom you are appealing; you must work up your concretized appeals. None of this can be done well—if done the last minute. To postpone is not only to miss the train—but to pay exorbitantly for the ticket for the train you missed. In the absence of planning, you get crisis action—a most familiar phenomenon around campaign headquarters: last minute expenditures, a mountain of debt, wasted money, literature and manpower.

Very often, the panic of a campaign is the product of the sloth of precampaign days. A good organization all 'round helps build a good organization in the campaign.

Election Day is the pay-off—but it is not the proof that your organization or your campaign were either good or bad. In a campaign, you need facts, funds, and footwork. It also helps if you have FATE. Many a political win is in the cards—no matter what you do. And many a political defeat is likewise in that same deal of the deck. The real test of your effort, your planning, your skill is in the election where the forces of fate are deadlocked and you —you alone, you with others—must make the final decision. Here it is that good campaigning, good organization, good personal work pays off. Maybe you—and your colleagues—are deciding only ten percent of the final outcome. The rest is determined by the force of fortune—for better or worse. But it is of that ten percent that politics is made—and so, too, in many cases is the fate of nations and peoples.

Once you have decided your probable audience, you are then faced with the joint problem of *themes* and *issues*. There is a good deal of difference of opinion on how to handle these matters, but Chotiner's advice is perhaps as good as there is.

> Now back to the theme. I have never believed in a slogan for a campaign. . . . The reason I never believe in a slogan for a campaign is because so many times the opposition may twist it or turn it.
>
> When I am talking about a theme, I am not talking about a slogan. I think we can have a theme without a slogan.
>
> Let me give you illustrations of themes. When Joe Holt became a candidate for Congress in California, we found he did not live in the district, and under the law you don't have to live in the Congressional District in order to run. The first thing Joe did was to rent an apartment in the district; he moved into the district, but his opponent did not. All through that campaign, all we had to keep on doing was to say that Joe Holt is "one of us" and that thing pyramided throughout the entire San Fernando Valley, and in Hollywood. Here was a candidate who thought enough of the district to live in the district, whereas the opponent did not.

As for following up a theme with issues, Chotiner—and nearly everyone else—recommends the following.

> May I suggest that at all times we restrict our issues to two instead of trying to cover the entire waterfront. That doesn't mean that we should not be prepared, if necessary, to answer questions that may be presented, but you cannot campaign on a multitude of issues. You have to pick two

or three issues at the outside to determine which are the ones you are going to be able to sell.

As this chapter is mainly devoted to the broad principles of campaigning, see the following chapter for some of the details involved in handling issues—and other matters—by individual candidates.

Moving beyond issues, there are the larger problems of *strategy and tactics*. Some ten of the most basic guidelines have been outlined by Miss Leone Baxter of the well-known public relations firm of Whitaker and Baxter, which has directed various types of political campaigns for nearly a quarter of a century. Characterized as "rules" for directing "in ethical, business-like fashion, campaigns for candidates, and campaigns for and against public issues," they have apparently served both the firm and its clients well. As Miss Baxter presented them some years ago before the Public Relations Society of America (see "Public Relations' Precocious Baby," *The Public Relations Journal*, January, 1950), they are—with paraphrased explanations—as follows.

1.   Fresh Air in the Finance Department. "Any bona fide committee, industry, or profession has the right to spend its own money to tell its story politically. But it has the concurrent obligation to report its expenditures publicly and accurately."

2.   Convictions Are Important. The firm does not attempt to direct campaigns which run counter to the principles the partners believe in.

3.   Don't Underestimate Your Opposition. Design your own campaign with all the skill you can muster, bearing in mind your opposition will do the same.

4.   Don't Underestimate the Man in the Street. He can do an excellent job of decision-making at election time if given a fair chance to hear both sides of the case.

5.   Mobilize Your Natural Allies. Don't neglect your friends and potential friends in your concern about your opposition.

6.   The Soundest Approach Is the Grass Roots Approach. "Get your story, your facts and your figures to the public

for study and for action. If your case stands up under such scrutiny, it will win public support."

7.   Stick to the Facts. Garbled facts and juggled figures have no place in a campaign seeking to win public support.

8.   You Can't Beat Something with Nothing. Defense is not enough. A constructive program and a positive appeal take a campaign out of the negative class, which holds little interest for the average voter.

9.   The Masses Are Also Individuals. Democrats and Republicans are also farmers, church members, veterans, and the like. Your story must be individualized as well as generalized.

10.   More Americans Like Corn than Caviar. Stick to simple language people can understand and dramatize what you have to say.

4. TIMETABLES

Finally, there is the important matter of *timetables*. So much in the organizational scheme of things depends on schedules. "Political skill," says Edward J. "Ed" Flynn, former National Chairman of the Democratic Party, "is mostly built on proper timing."

There is, however, no mathematical formula by which timing can be controlled. There are too many things to take into account. But a political campaign of any kind must proceed according to some plan—all of which builds up the campaign to the final climax, the election.

This plan will, first, depend upon the official election timetable, known as the *election calendar*. This is usually published as a small pamphlet under the auspices of the secretary of state in your state. It is based on the legal requirements concerning such things as the last day for absent voters' applications, the last day for submitting nomination petitions, the last day for naming persons to election duties, and the like. Election calendars and guides are especially important for persons who may wish to get on the ballot and to obtain nominations for public office. As ballots and election materials must be printed beforehand, certain time limits have been set for candidates and proposals. These time limits must be observed or you will not even get started.

In other words, if you want to get on the ballot or get something on it, study the state election laws and election calendar before you leap. Follow the rules—with the advice of a lawyer if possible—and then carry through in accord with your state's time schedule.

Once you know the official schedule, you can then prepare your own schedule of political events designed to put across your program.

However, if you are not experienced at these things, you may leave something out. To remedy such oversights the Republican National Committee has outlined a suggested timetable for a November election. Taken from the committee's *Campaign Manual*, this is one of the most complete examples of its kind—in many ways almost a full campaign guide in itself, which is a main reason for its inclusion here in such detail.

However, if you are in a small district where campaigning is minimal, do not let this checklist bother you. Run through it and select what you feel is appropriate for you and your situation, and let the rest go.

Campaign Timetable

FOR A NOVEMBER ELECTION

MAY–SEPTEMBER 15; PLANNING THE CAMPAIGN:

1. Select the campaign manager, publicity chairman, and treasurer.

2. Circulate petitions and obtain the necessary signatures for nomination of the candidate.

3. Start the research committee and put it into high gear immediately. Work out your basic thinking on the expected campaign issues and basic campaign strategy; plan your campaign literature. If possible, write basic speeches.

4. Select the campaign headquarters and open it as

soon as possible. Procure furniture, equipment, type-writers, office supplies, etc.

5. Recruit the headquarters secretary; start to recruit division chairmen and key figures, and begin the recruiting phase generally. Print or mimeograph Workers' Cards in two colors, if possible.

6. Obtain a good map and make necessary photostatic copies.

SEPTEMBER 15; STARTING OPERATIONS:

1. Step up research; candidate should complete his education on all aspects of the campaign and get his speech-writing well under way.

2. Start the publicity program; put it in high gear and keep it there; obtain personnel; plan speeches, releases, press conferences, etc.; co-ordinate activities of research and publicity.

3. Start canvassing program; obtain voters' lists; print or mimeograph voters' cards, recruit regional and precinct captains; divide precincts up into regions; emphasize building up precinct units; consider separate apartment house program; start telephone canvass.

4. Start the speaking program; start to recruit would-be speakers; plan, obtain, or start writing canned speeches; start grouping would-be speakers into teams; make up inside meetings calendar and start inside speaking program.

5. Print or mimeograph literature drop cards; draft affirmative literature and posters. Start literature drop file.

6. Start the candidate's personal program; make up the candidate's calendar; start personal appearances; stimulate contacts with groups, organizations, etc.

7. Start the receptionist program.

8. Consider plans for rallies, caravans, and parades.

9. Start the poll-watching program, begin preparation of the poll-watchers' manual.

10. Start fund raising.

11. Establish any necessary liaison with the regular party organization.

OCTOBER 1; THE EXCITEMENT INCREASES:

1. Start mimeographing research memoranda, discussing the candidates, issues, opponent's voting record, etc., in detail. Make them available to all workers. You will be surprised how far they will go on their own if they are good. People want *facts*. Issue more as the campaign progresses and opportunity affords. Save the stencils for reprinting.

2. Print one good piece of affirmative literature, setting forth the candidate's qualifications; use good paper; make it a masterpiece; instruct the printer to hold type for possible reprinting; distribute to all campaign workers for further distribution and watch how it goes. Print and distribute posters.

3. Reappraise and intensify publicity program and step it up if possible.

4. Step up canvassing; concentrate on organizing the canvassing operation and recruiting its workers; start canvassing of voters on an experimental basis.

5. Step up the speakers' program; distribute canned speeches; construct soapboxes; print placards; form teams; start practice sessions; step up recruiting; plan sound-truck program.

6. Crystallize plans for rallies, caravans, parades. Step up fund raising.

7. Select chairman, special services division.

8. Step up work on draft of poll-watchers' manual; make plans for printing or mimeographing it; start planning details of poll-watching on election day; establish liaison with state attorney general's office.

OCTOBER 10; JUST BEFORE THE FIREWORKS:

1. Start general canvassing of voters; step up recruiting of block captains, additional canvassers, etc. Build up precinct units.

2. Complete preparation for speakers' operation. Send out enthusiastic speakers for first street-corner engagements. Complete training and practice sessions of others. Select locations for outside meetings; complete sound-truck arrangements.

3. Recruit literature distribution teams to go with

speakers' teams; work up literature drop file; start addressing envelopes for mailing; consider issuing additional literature.

4. Gear special services to canvassing.

5. Step up the receptionist program.

6. Reappraise and step up the candidate's personal program; add to the buffer team if necessary.

7. Complete plans for rallies, meetings, caravans, parades.

8. Complete the poll-watchers' manual; make plans for poll-watchers' instruction meetings.

Two Weeks Before Election; The Guns Go Off:

1. The canvassing program moves into high gear; all canvassers go out; step up recruiting; step up telephone canvass plans for election day.

2. The speakers' program moves into high gear, all outside teams go to locations; send out sound trucks.

3. Literature distributors' program moves into high gear; LTD's go with speakers' teams to busy street corners; send literature out by mail.

4. Receptionist program moves into high gear.

5. Complete plans for the poll-watching program; send the poll-watchers' manual to all prospective poll-watchers, with letter asking that it be studied, and scheduling poll-watchers' instruction meetings.

6. Step up general recruiting.

7. Get the candidate to bed early.

Last Week Before Election; Up and At 'Em:

1. Keep up recruiting generally.

2. Step up all operations, canvassing, telephone canvass, speakers, literature distribution. Send out sample ballots and consider issuing additional literature. Send out additional sound trucks.

3. Put on major rally.

4. As election day nears, put on parades, caravans; step up meetings and the general agitation.

5. Campaign manager must watch expenses. Gear disbursements to income.

6. Complete poll-watching program and election day assignments.

7. Reappraise candidate's personal program; enable the candidate to avoid fatigue and be at his best. Don't bother him with any more details than absolutely necessary.

On Election Day; Watch the Polls:

1. Distribute sample ballots and literature to voters approaching the polls.

2. Don't let them steal the vote.

3. Victory.

4. Victory party at headquarters for workers and friends.

6. CONCLUSION

A timetable such as the above—or lesser ones—should be carefully planned, but you must be prepared to shift and change with the tempo of events. If it is to be effective, it can never be a completely static thing.

Chapter 10

On Being a Candidate

Intertwined throughout the general organization are the requirements and problems of individual candidates. Many of these have been touched on in the previous chapters; in this discussion some of them will be considered in greater detail. We will cover:

1. *the requirements for candidacy*, particularly those of a personal nature;
2. *getting started*, including the nomination process;
3. *handling the candidate*, from the standpoint of those managing his campaign; and some
4. *tactics and tips* for the conduct of the campaign.

Again, the literature on candidates is full of all sorts of miscellaneous recommendations. Here, it is possible only to hit the high spots, recognizing that on many matters there may be omissions or differences of opinion, particularly with respect to special situations.

1. IF YOU WANT TO BE A CANDIDATE

In his autobiography, *Adventures in Politics*, the late Senator Richard L. Neuberger of Oregon has an appendix titled "Politics—and You." "Perhaps you are worried," he writes, "about your age, your religion, your physical appearance, a skeleton in the family closet, or about the limited time you went to school. It could be that you have thought seriously of being a candidate for office in your state or local community and then abandoned the idea because of some handicap, real or imagined."

If these matters concern you, you should look up Neuberger's chapter. For in it the author discusses some 35 personal problems of the sort he mentions above, varying from "What If I'm a Woman?" to "Will a Foreign Name Hurt My Chances?" Actually, candidates have been successful with almost every conceivable qualification or disqualification.

Nevertheless, there are some general principles to consider. These have been stated most forthrightly by Murray Chotiner, again in a section of his 1955 talk on the "Fundamentals of Campaign Organization." Certainly, if you cannot meet these qualifications—often termed "the four 'C's' "—your chances are going to be considerably lessened.

> . . . I think every winning candidate, generally speaking, must have these four attributes.
>
> In the first place, he must be *clean*, and by clean I mean his record, his background, and his own personal life, because—remember this—the things that we don't know about our own candidate, the opposition either knows or will find out. You can rest assured that they will hit at them some time during the course of the campaign.
>
> The second attribute is that he must be *clear*, and I mean clear on the issues. Too many times our candidates speak on both sides and half the time you can't be sure

just which stand they are taking. But you can't fool the voting public. They catch on mighty quickly.

Third, he must be *constructive*. Why? Because people want to know whether your candidate stands for something. If he only picks out one thing that he is going to advocate, let us go up and down the state and district and indicate that this is something that he believes in and something for which he is going to work.

Then the fourth attribute of the candidate; he must be *courageous*, and by courageous, I mean he must be willing to put on a fighting campaign. The people like a fighter, and if you ever get a candidate who is a Milquetoast and won't get out and fight, the odds are that he is going to be defeated.

Let us assume now that you meet Chotiner's specifications and someone seriously proposes you as a candidate. Should you accept? At this point consider a warning issued in 1964 by the Republican City Committee of Boston. "Step 1" of the Committee's *Road to Victory*, a general guide for candidates, is as follows.

When a person becomes a candidate for public office, he runs the risk of losing. If the situation were otherwise, many more people would seek to become candidates. Many elections are lost because a candidate is unwilling to commit himself fully to the pursuit of victory, fearing loss of face if he is defeated in spite of an all-out effort. Such people are constantly on the defensive, apologizing for their lack of courage with such comments as: "I merely ran as a favor to the party" or "I let them use my name." Whether or not you think you have a chance of winning, are running to help other GOP candidates, or simply want to get some things off your chest, you have a responsibility, as long as you are a candidate, to commit yourself totally to the pursuit of victory: a responsibility to yourself, to those aiding you in your campaign, and to every Republican voter in your district. If you are not a serious candidate, save the time, money, energy, and dedication of all concerned by making that fact perfectly clear—and don't waste your time reading further. There is no shame in waging a valiant fight against long odds, win or lose. The real failure is the person who lacks the guts to try.

The first step on the road to victory is commitment. It must be total. Once it is made, it cannot be withdrawn. You can't play Hamlet in politics.

So you have faced the issue and accepted. You agree to become a candidate, a fighting candidate!

Now, what about your image? As to whether or not you should "be yourself" as a candidate, most observers say "Yes." Along with Chotiner, they advise that "where you have weaknesses in your candidate, you should take advantage of them."

> As an illustration—when Joe Holt ran for Congress in Los Angeles County, a veteran of the Korean war, only twenty-six years old, the people said he was too young. "You don't want to send a young fellow twenty-six years of age to Congress. What experience has he had?" We could not hide the fact that he was twenty-six. We capitalized on it. We told the people of his district that what the district needs is a young man to go back to Congress and make those old-timers sit up and take notice. We need somebody who has the vim and vitality to go to Washington and do a job, and Joe Holt became the Congressman from that district.

By all means improve your delivery in public speaking, and try to remember names better. But, as former Senator William Knowland of California is reported to have said, when his advisers told him he would have to change his personality, "Well, you know, you may be right. But that is the way I happen to be. If you start changing me, you are apt to get a worse product than when you started."

Then, too, you must often consider the needs and views of the regular party organization and just where you might fit in. Do you have the qualifications from the *party* point of view? One such view which is fairly representative is that found in the New York Democratic State Committee's *Handbook for Campaign Workers.*

The Candidate

The candidate carries the party banner in the election. The man or woman picked for that honor was chosen for one of several reasons. Assuming that he properly represents the party's standards of public service and is well-qualified for the office, he may be selected because victory is sure and it is desired to reward a faithful party member for past services; he may be picked because he has a particular following that he may be able to rally to his and the party's cause; he may be chosen for the purely practical reason that he is judged to have the best chance of winning what looks like a close contest; or he may be chosen because he is willing to go down to defeat, in a hopeless cause, just for the party's sake.

In any of these contingencies, the party has a definite obligation to the candidate to help him with his campaign and get for him every conceivable vote.

In a well-run organization, there always should be plenty of available candidates. The party chairman has encouraged young men to seek party posts, and he has never closed his door to a budding statesman. If the aspirant has ability and is loyal to the party cause, the chairman can build him up, by gradual promotion, to being an asset for the party and the chairman. To treat the party as a closed corporation, and every newcomer as a potential rival, would lead to factionalism, party discord, and a shortage of men to carry the party label in victory or defeat.

It is often good tactics to pick candidates a year in advance, thus heading off primary fights and also giving plenty of time for the "building-up" of the designee for a particular office. The "build-up" process is one that can easily become neglected. But experience has shown that the public reacts best to a familiar name, one that it recognizes as having done things in and for the community. The candidate who does not have to be introduced to the electorate when he runs for office is apt to make the best showing.

If you meet all the qualifications outlined in this section—or a reasonable proportion of them—then perhaps you are ready to start. Where, then, do you begin?

2. GETTING STARTED

The AFL-CIO political action manual, *How to Win*, recommends that "if you do encourage a person to run for public office start him off with the less important elections."

> Your project is a long-term one—and should be. Get him to run for county commissioner. Get him to run for the school board or the public service commission. These elections serve both to give him campaign experience and to get him known. In addition you are making a contribution to your community by encouraging good, honest citizens to run for public office.
>
> But don't underestimate the importance of the Board of Education or the City Council. These are vital and important functions in themselves, worthy of a full-time political career. They should never be regarded mere stepping stones to the legislature or Congress.

On the whole this is good advice. Any candidacy, however, involves some sort of nominating process. Here we come back to caucuses and primaries. It is in caucuses that the initial selections are often made, for it is there that the party organization often makes up its mind about whom to support later in the primaries.

But both involve nominations, about which there is something more to be said, for any candidate must first attempt to obtain a nomination for some public office. Here he inevitably runs into election law and procedure, which can sometimes be rather sticky.

The following paragraph from the *Handbook for Campaign Workers* of the Democratic State Committee of New York contains some good advice.

> The election law provisions governing petition-gathering and -signing are rigid and technical, with the Boards

of Election and the courts showing a consistent tendency to hold would-be nominees to the letter of the law. It can not be stressed too much that the local law chairman supervise all petitions and be called in to settle any point in doubt. Corner-cutting and chance-taking may result in the candidate not getting even as far as the primary ballot.

If you obtain the nomination finally, then there is the problem of a full campaign. Your nomination attempt will have got you started, of course, but only in a preliminary way. Much that has been discussed in the previous chapter now fully applies. Your campaign manager has been selected, and "the organization" is in full swing.

To some extent you, as a candidate, will be in control. But more and more you will become "the managed"; hence the next topic.

3. HANDLING THE CANDIDATE

Here is the advice of the Republican National Committee on how to manage the affairs of a candidate for public office, as described in its *Campaign Manual*.

A Candidate is like a Race Horse

Once a man consents to run for public office, he becomes more than a mere individual. He becomes a public character, an advocate and a symbol of certain ideas of public concern. His essential job is to sell those ideas to the public; and that means that he must perform before the public in personal appearances of all kinds.

Thus a candidate is like a race horse. He, too, must run his race in front of the public. And he, too, needs a considerable amount of preparation, assistance, and "handling," in order to run a good race.

So every campaign manager should regard his candidate with what might be described as a cool, professional eye, in order to give him all the assistance necessary to perform well before the public. To that end it is ordinarily essential for the campaign manager to organize a candidate's personal program in order to make the most out of his personal appearances.

The Problems of Personal Appearances

Every candidate is confronted, and sometimes deluged, with requests for speaking engagements, appearances at meetings, parties, dinners, receptions, etc. Each request must be handled politely and diplomatically. And if the candidate attends, additional problems arise. There is a substantial transportation problem, for speeches sometimes have to be given in remote or outlandish places.

If he should lose his copy of a written speech, he may be in serious trouble. He may want to make a telephone call while at the meeting, or there may be a telephone call for him. Messengers may appear, or the candidate may want to send a message. All these facts make it essential that he be afforded personal assistance in every aspect of appearing before the public.

A Candidate's Personal Program

Definite responsibility should be placed upon some individual for coordinating the candidate's personal program. Since much of this is daytime work, a woman is often a suitable choice for the position of coordinator, and the individual should preferably be given a desk and telephone at the campaign headquarters.

MAKE UP A CALENDAR

A candidate's calendar should be made up at the outset of the campaign, containing a full, separate page for every day of the campaign through election day. Morning engagements should be written in at the top, luncheon engagements near the middle, afternoon and evening engagements toward the bottom, and the type of transportation should be stated, with other details. As engagements are made, the candidate will, of course, be consulted, and the secretary in his business office should maintain a duplicate of the candidate's calendar. The candidate's calendar will tell the candidate at a glance of his commitments and the details, and will prevent broken engagements, misunderstandings, and the resultant catastrophes.

MAKING ENGAGEMENTS

Requests

All requests which come in should be referred initially to the coordinator of the candidate's personal program. He or she should obtain all the pertinent information, and then consult the candidate or his business secretary. That will save the candidate time and embarrassment, enable the coordinator to screen the requests, and see that each gets adequate consideration.

Stimulating Engagements

A good coordinator can also stimulate requests for engagements. The candidate or the campaign organization usually has affiliations with various organizations, rotary and business clubs, ethnic and minority groups, social groups, etc. The coordinator should ascertain these; and he or she will then find that a friendly telephone call to the key person in the club or group will often result in a request for the candidate to appear by that organization or club, either to speak, or simply to make a personal appearance and meet the members. These contacts are of very great value.

Use of the Literature Drop File

The coordinator should keep abreast of the literature drop file at headquarters and use the contacts listed as a basis for stimulating requests, where possible. Many of these individuals and organizations would like to see the candidate, but are hesitant to suggest it.

KEEPING ENGAGEMENTS: THE BUFFER TEAM

Take Mechanical Problems Off the Candidate's Hands

As pointed out above, keeping engagements involves many mechanical problems for every candidate, e.g., transportation, telephone calls, messages, finding the place, getting there on time, etc. A group of two or three persons, or at least one person, should always accompany the candidate on every engagement to handle these mechanical problems for him, as a buffer team. One person should act as its captain on every occasion.

Transportation

Transportation facilities can be provided by people willing to lend the use of their automobiles for transportation of the candidate on a definite schedule fitting the candidate's calendar. One or two persons should go along in the car with the candidate, besides the driver. People are often glad to volunteer for that type of work, as it is highly entertaining and carries the prestige of accompanying the candidate. They should be carefully chosen, for people tend to judge the candidate by the type of people who are with him.

The job of the buffer team captain in connection with transportation is to see that the candidate has transportation for every engagement that he wants to attend, and does not have to worry about obtaining it, parking, etc. He should also see that the candidate arrives at every engagement on time, that he leaves on time, and that he arrives at the next place on time.

At Meetings, and Parties, etc.

The job of the buffer team at all meetings, parties, dinners, etc., is to handle telephone calls, messages, and errands for the candidate; to see that everyone who wants to meet the candidate has a chance to do so, and that he is not monopolized by an ardent conversationalist. They should bring people at the meeting up to the candidate, so as to give them a chance to shake hands with and talk to the candidate. The candidate can seldom take this initiative on himself, and most people at the meeting will be reluctant to advance upon him. Members of the buffer team should always act as intermediaries and break the ice. It will add greatly to the friendly spirit of the meeting.

When the candidate travels to distant places, it is helpful to obtain one or more local people to serve on the buffer team, so that they can advise on local problems and people.

Fatigue

The public always expects leadership, if not inspiration, from a political candidate. That means that everything he says and does before the public should make sense and exude leadership. To do that, the candidate must not allow himself to become fatigued. He cannot inspire or lead anybody's thinking if he is tired. Hence, one purpose of the buffer team is to enable the candidate to avoid fatigue.

They should make sure that he gets to bed at reasonable hours. People usually urge a candidate to stay at a meeting or party, and may be offended if he personally insists on breaking away. But a member of the buffer team can insist that the candidate go, in order not to disappoint people at a subsequent engagement, and thus remove from the candidate any embarrassment on breaking away.

RECRUITMENT OF WORKERS

Enthusiastic supporters for the candidate will materialize at almost every meeting, party, dinner, etc. Those enthusiasts should be recruited as workers on the spot by the buffer team; for after the meeting it may be impossible to get the names and addresses.

In addition, the AFL-CIO manual, *How to Win*, thoughtfully recommends some special attention to the candidate's personal office in the headquarters.

The Candidate's Office

The candidate's room should again have information charts, maps, reference books, etc.

In addition remember your candidate is constantly on the go and will appreciate a chance to wash up or rest in his room. If you possibly can, give him a couch and an office with running water, towels, etc. . . . His office should provide maximum comfort and privacy. He will need quiet to study and prepare speeches and for interviews. Therefore his office should be as far removed from the noisy humdrum as possible.

Finally, what about a candidate's wife? The Democratic National Committee has available, for example, a small flyer containing *Tips for Candidate's Wives*. Above all, the Committee advises, "Be natural."

> Nothing is so distracting from the good impression you wish to make as affectation. Don't be afraid to be yourself. Tell yourself: "I am an individual; my mannerisms, my physical characteristics, and my background mark my individuality. I shall not imitate another's mannerisms, for I would lose all that makes me an interesting, personable being." Do not let anyone talk you into doing something in which you would feel uncomfortable or unnatural. Find your role, and play it!

As part of a School for Candidates on April 4, 1964, the Republican State Committee of Pennsylvania held a "Special Session for Wives of Candidates." In a preparatory handout entitled *Petticoat Politics for Political Partners*, both "home-body" and "energetic" types can find some suggestions.

> If you're the *home-body* type, don't fret, you can be as important as the gad-about. Here are some pointers on how:
> 1. Attend to home chores usually done by your husband.
> 2. See that he relaxes when he is home, which won't be often.
> 3. Be an expert packer.
> 4. Be a good sounding board, let him blow off steam to you and try out new ideas.
> 5. Keep an accurate record of messages.
> 6. Be a home secretary, answer invitations and write thank-you notes promptly.
> 7. Read local papers, listen to newscasts and generally keep up-to-date politically.
> 8. Don't beg your candidate husband to stay home more. If he is at home, make sure he hasn't forgot a meeting, and it isn't all a mistake.
> 9. Try to go to some of the women's meetings which are in the daytime generally.
> 10. Do attend a few functions with your husband or rumors will start that your marriage is unhappy.
> Some suggestions for *energetic you:*

1. Be equally nice to everyone, no favorites.
2. When you speak, be brief, turn the spotlight on "him."
3. Listen when your husband speaks publicly. Laugh at his jokes even though it's the tenth time you've heard them.
4. Be enthusiastic, enjoy yourself and enter wholeheartedly into meetings.
5. Good grooming is vital, everyone is looking at you.
6. Be a traveling secretary and nurse, take notes and aspirin and remember names.
7. Develop a thick skin and don't let criticism upset you. If it's constructive accept it, otherwise forget it.
8. Go to women's meetings on your own, Kaffee Klatches, teas, etc. Talk to everyone about your favorite man.
9. Carry a camera and take pictures of your husband and friends on the campaign trail.
10. Always put "him" in the spotlight. Use husband's name on name tags. Just remember he is the candidate, not you!

There are other problems involving the candidate, but all that can be said here is that the candidate must be kept in mind in almost every type of organizational activity. Canvassers, speakers, committee members, and other party workers must be familiar with each candidate's record and adjust their efforts accordingly—cooperating to the best of their ability with whatever special managers or clubs or committees may be devoting their time entirely to that candidate.

4. TACTICS AND TIPS

Among the first decisions which a candidate and his manager are likely to have to make is that concerning where the candidate can best spend his time in public. Should the campaign emphasize large, public gatherings or small, more intimate meetings and conferences?

The relative merits of these two alternatives have been

covered well by James E. Downes of the New Jersey State Teachers College in Newark, himself a former candidate for Congress, in his booklet, *Grass-roots Politics*.

Do Campaign Speeches "Pay Off?"

The campaign speech is usually regarded (even by some experienced politicians) as the key factor in pre-election activities. Yet its value in winning votes is to be doubted very seriously. The evidence seems to indicate that the best way for a candidate to gain the support of the uncommitted is to arrange to meet them in very small groups, to chat with them informally, to give them a chance to ask him questions. Before the election, he should travel about the district, "getting together" here and there with a few voters at the corner drugstore, on buses, in the park, at a ball game. If his "just folks" technique is functioning properly and if he is prepared to answer all the embarrassing questions that may be asked, he will materially increase his chances of being elected, even if he never makes a speech, except for a few "musts" at major party rallies.

This method of campaigning has worked successfully for an increasing number of candidates in recent years. There are, perhaps, two major reasons for its effectiveness: (1) People have become more and more skeptical of political speeches. Even on the comparatively few occasions when they can be persuaded to attend a meeting and listen to a speech, they take what they hear with a liberal helping of salt. (2) The average person gets so little direct personal attention these days from individuals in public life that when one flatters him by a personal call and talk, he is likely to vote for him out of sheer gratitude.

Granted a decision on the problem above, there then arises the question of what to talk about. This is the matter of "issues" again. In their book, *Going Into Politics*, Robert E. Merriam and Rachel M. Goetz have made the following prescription for "legislators" and "citizen lobbyists," which applies equally well to almost all public figures, including candidates:

1. *Know your issue*. Never enter a debate unless you know what you are talking about. Does this sound too elementary? Read any legislative journal, even the *Congressional Record*, and you will be amazed to see how often this elementary precaution is ignored. This rule also applies to appearances before legislative or administrative committees. How one cringes for the individual pleading a good cause who is led to slaughter when his lack of preparation is laid bare! Of all the weaknesses demonstrated by civic organizations in their dealings with government bodies, inadequate preparation and presentation lead the rest.

2. *Establish priorities*. Whether legislator, administrator, or citizen, one must exercise selectivity. Too many balls in the air at the same time diffuse interest and attention and important matters may get lost. Pick the issues important to you and fight for them one at a time.

3. *Plan your attack*. Every public issue, no matter what its virtues, needs to have its way prepared. This is important. If, for example, the issue is a higher minimum hourly wage, get national columnists, economists, professional groups, legislators, administrators, and citizen organizations thinking about the matter before you move.

4. *Stick to the essentials*. Organize your case so that it can be understood by the lowest common denominator of your potential support. Be clear and precise; leave out interesting but extraneous sidelights. Many a good idea has gone down the drain when its proponents fell into the trap of becoming involved in lengthy arguments about inconsequential details

5. *Dramatize your issue*. Do not be a sensationalist, but remember that what you have to say must compete with many other interests, some of which may be dramatic. So be factual but interesting. Solid showmanship is important.

6. *Be persistent*. Many a promising campaign has foundered because its supporters gave up when success was almost in sight. Remember that everything takes time, especially in politics, and cultivate the necessary patience to put over your program. The economy bloc in the Chicago City Council pounded away year after year at

certain vulnerable spots in the city budget until they finally forced action. It was a long pull; 101 amendments involving six million dollars were proposed, but only one item for thirteen dollars was passed in the first year. Three years later, however, more than one-half of the savings originally proposed were in effect. And since then still others have been acted upon. The seeds of good ideas are tough and germinal.

As the campaign develops, the opposition will begin to make itself felt. If you are attacked, how should you reply? The formula outlined below has been specifically designed by the National Municipal League for civic associations, but it applies equally well to anyone involved in campaigning. It comes from the League's manual, *The Citizen Association: How To Win Civic Campaigns*.

Answering the Opposition

One thing that citizen campaigners can count on is an attack by the opposition. Virtually every campaign steps on the toes of persons who have a vested interest in keeping oldfashioned government or preserving their own jobs or spending public money for private benefit.

The opposition often becomes desperate as the threat of a citizen victory looms greater. Desperate men will make any kind of accusation and resort to any kind of trick. Some of the worst slanders will be whispered, but others will appear in newspaper stories and in literature.

GET A LOAD OF THIS

Citizen campaigners who wouldn't touch a Communist with a 10-foot pole have been described as pinks and reds. Conscientious administrators have been labeled dictators. Ousted politicians who once flourished on graft have charged their honest successors with juggling tax assessments for their own benefit. Men and women who have not sought public office have been called political climbers.

A commonly circulated tale in council-manager charter campaigns is that the charter advocates a plan to import some outsider at an absurd salary to be dictator of the local government. Another rumor is that the new manager will immediately dismiss hundreds of faithful city employees.

In a New Jersey city, the established politicians warned the Negro voters that most city managers come from southern states and a Jim Crow regime could be expected. The same politicians passed the word among white voters that employment of a city manager would increase the number of Negroes in city jobs.

Political organizations have long controlled elections through the votes of city employees, their families and friends. Municipal employees are sensitive to any threat to their security. Citizen campaigners should therefore give extra attention to this group. They should beat the regular politicians to the punch by distributing a special folder that will tell how the new charter or proposed merit system will improve security and working conditions in local government. Examples of gains in other cities will be persuasive, especially when pay raises are cited.

The key to successful countering of your opponents' charges is to anticipate the attack and get your story to the voters first. Plan a campaign that is both constructive and honest. If you wish to get rid of the hack whose handling of tax assessments has long been notorious, say so. At the same time you can promise that every city employee who is willing to perform an honest day's work can feel secure.

KEEP ON THE OFFENSIVE

The voters will like you better if your attitude is one of complete frankness. Major attacks from the opposition should get straightforward and immediate replies and then be ignored. Don't let your opponents put you on the defensive by keeping you busy answering their statements. Show them that this tactic will boomerang because you will counterattack every time. For example, you will dispose of the accusation in a paragraph or two and then say, in effect: "This phony charge will not divert the attention of the voters from the real issue: Why has the municipal budget increased 74 percent in six years while salaries have gone up only 22 percent, no schools have been built, streets have been neglected, the water system is leaking and nothing has been done to solve the traffic problem?"

An indictment of this kind, used over and over again, can be deadly. It is handy for keeping the campaign on the offensive and away from the defensive, which is the place where the opposition belongs.

THE SNEAK ATTACK

Often the opposition, at first discounting the power of a citizen group and then confronted with the possibility of defeat, will hold its fire until the last few days of the campaign. It will then unleash a slanderous barrage via newspaper advertisements, radio and television, leaflets or other media. Some civic campaigns have been demoralized by these unexpected, last-minute attacks.

The primary defense against this tactic is, as already explained, a campaign that anticipates the opposition and disposes of its charges before they are made.

The second line of defense is preparedness. Be prepared with the text of a full-page newspaper ad for the day before election, and be prepared to revise the text if necessary to answer last-minute charges. Be prepared with a reservation of radio time. It is even possible to arrange with a cooperative printer for weekend production of a leaflet that can be distributed house-to-house the day before election.

And don't forget the telephone. Your volunteers should be prepared to make thousands of calls, if necessary, to reassure voters listed in your card file as sympathetic, and to remind them to vote.

The chances of a last-minute surprise attack will be minimized if you use your block organization as a good intelligence service.

Finally, there are all the miscellaneous "dos and don'ts" for which there are innumerable prescriptions. But a short list of fundamentals has been outlined by Gus Tyler in the Americans for Democratic Action handbook, *Voting Guide, 1956.* This list is as good as any and has the additional merit of being short enough that you can hope to remember it.

Once you are the candidate—having entered the lists and won the primary—the greatest service you can do for yourself is to make yourself known. Here are some suggestions:

1. If you can help it, never mention your opponent. Imagine a Lucky Strike ad that consisted mainly of saying, "Don't Smoke Chesterfields." Your average listener will probably miss much of your argument and remember nothing but the word Chesterfields. When he goes to buy, the brand name will come to his lips automatically. Many voters act the same way when they must choose from many names at the bottom of the list. Keep your name in the forefront.

2. In the three or four months before Election Day, stay within the boundaries of your district. This is a dramatic way of saying that you should not lose a minute in ploughing, seeding, watering, tending your backyard —your own district!

3. Save money on meeting halls by using people's homes. There are many ways of getting to people in their homes. Try a house-to-house canvass. Try it with your husband or wife. Try house parties, arranged by your backers. They invite friends and neighbors to meet you socially. A speech is not totally out of order, if people demand it and if it's short.

4. Visit your shopping centers: groceries, pharmacies, butcher shop, five-and-dime. The smaller the place, the better. Ask people what they think, what they want, and tell them why you are interested.

5. In presenting yourself to people, get it out of your head that you, as a candidate, must become the stereotype of a candidate. Be yourself. If there is a nasty and a pleasant side of yourself, try to show the nice side. But don't try to be somebody else—a stuffed shirt, a wind-bag. Somehow people sense a phony, especially

when they meet him personally. In a long and energetic campaign, you will also find it much less wearing to be yourself than to be somebody else.

Don't expect to get elected the first time you run. This is especially true if you represent something different and are not just a name slipped into the lot by the forces-that-be in your district. You should act as if you expect to win, but don't really count on it. Look upon the first campaign as an investment in the second.

After your first campaign—win or lose—let your backers know that you are really indebted to them for their backing. You are, you know. Let them know it, honestly, deeply and personally.

The real army is formed in the battle. Hold it together. Many a defeat is the crucible in which are forged the weapons for victory.

5. CONCLUSION

While this chapter has dealt mainly with the problems of a candidate while he is running for office, it is not too much to say that a politician is always running for office. A candidate's problems only commence with his mastery of his first election. He then must almost immediately begin to think about the next one.

Chapter 11

Publicity
and
Salesmanship

The final test of any political organization must be: Are the issues getting to the voters with any impact? Organizations and candidates are as good as the elections they win.

An election campaign, like any attempt to influence public opinion, is a complex thing. Everything seems to go on all at once. In a book, about the best that can be done is to single out some of the most important aspects of the selling side of campaigning and describe them one after the other. The ways of mixing them up to support a candidate are endless. It will be possible here to outline only tentative guidelines.

Some political action techniques related to publicity and salesmanship have already been discussed. See especially the section of Chapter 6 which deals with recruiting, and some of the fund-raising devices in Chapter 7. Person-to-person and door-to-door types of political activity, as well as use of the telephone, are covered in the next chapter.

Here we will be concerned mainly with the so-called "mass media." These are the ones we usually think of when we speak of "publicity." They will be discussed under these headings:

1. *the public relations job*, including the organizational dimensions of the task;
2. *printed materials*, particularly those relating to news, advertising, handouts, and the like;
3. *radio and television;* and
4. *rallies, meetings, and related techniques.*

Of course, such a brief discussion as this will not in itself make you competent at public relations. But it should give you some idea of what to expect and where to begin. If you really want to get into the fine points of these affairs, then you had better engage a public relations counsel or an advertising agency.

1. THE PUBLICITY JOB

As all public relations is so closely intertwined with campaigning, the ultimate *organizational responsibility* must lie with the candidate and, especially, his campaign manager. However, the details of public relations, as they involve various media, are too complex to be supervised effectively by one person or, often, even by one committee.

It is customary to divide up the public relations job among several chairmen or committees, all operating under the general guidance of the manager and his overall strategy committee. Such an arrangement, for a quite populous area, might envisage a general Publicity Chairman with separate committees for public relations (press), advertising, radio and TV, literature preparation, speakers, and meetings.

More typical is the two-man (or two-committee) arrangement currently favored by the Democratic National Committee, and suitable for a medium-sized city or county campaign. As outlined in the 1964 *Democratic Campaign Handbook*, a press secretary and an advertising agency form the backbone of the campaign publicity effort. The functions of each have been described as follows:

Press Secretary

No matter what he's called—publicity chairman, press agent, press secretary—this is the person who prepares news announcements and stories, distributes them to the press (including radio and television) and generally acts as a liaison between the candidate and the press.

Small, local campaigns may have to make do with a well-intentioned volunteer with little or no newswriting experience. (In this kind of campaign, participants should write the Democratic National Committee for a copy of "Campaign Communications Handbook" which is full of useful information particularly helpful to volunteer publicity workers.)

If the campaign can afford it—and every campaign from Congressional up should be able to afford it—a professional should handle press relations.

If the campaign is for a relatively minor office, the part-time services of a public relations firm or free-lance writer with a press background and political sensitivity may suffice.

In any case, the campaign director should get the best person the budget can stand. Ideally the person should have a solid background in newspaper, radio or television reporting, know the key press people, be a quick and accurate writer, be able to adapt his writing to suit the candidate's personal style, and be willing to put in the long hours and travel time the job requires.

He must become familiar with procedures for getting releases to newspapers and stations on time, the deadlines for the weekly newspapers, the importance of foreign-language and other small publications, and the need for creating a feeling of trust and mutual respect with members of the press.

The press secretary should have a working arrangement with a photographer who will take sufficient interesting and colorful pictures of the candidate to use in brochures, tabloids, mailers, and other pieces of campaign literature, as well as service the press.

Someone in the campaign organization, preferably the campaign director, should have specific authority and responsibility for clearing *all* press releases issued in the candidate's name, and no release should be distributed without this person's approval. A press release batted out under the pressure of a campaign deadline can inadvertently contain a statement (or misstatement) that will come back to haunt the candidate. To repeat, *all* press releases should be cleared before release.

The press secretary also should give the candidate and campaign director guidance on the preparation of statements and position papers. He may be able to write speeches, and work with the advertising agency in the preparation of brochures and other campaign materials.

Among the other specific responsibilities of the press secretary are these:

Work closely with the Democratic National Committee in distributing, throughout his area, news and policy statements. . . .

Keep a tight check on the news-gathering activities of the opponent, and determine how the candidate and his opponent are treated in the various media.

Maintain a clipping service of all statements, photographs, advertisements, and articles about the candidate and his opponent. In this area, as in others, he must work closely with the research chairman.

Stay in close touch with all newspaper, radio and television newsmen. Most of the time he will represent the candidate to these important people. A workable, cordial relationship is essential.

Publicize in advance the appearance of a member of the national Democratic ticket or other Democratic candidates or spokesmen visiting the area.

Publicize dinners, parties, and other events where the candidate will appear.

Prepare and clear for release endorsements of the candidate by various groups and individuals.

Working with the campaign director, the press secretary must be certain local publicity chairmen are appointed, encouraged and supervised. Without them, secondary campaign events, such as local activities of special groups, will pass unnoticed.

Advertising Counsel

There are many advantages to hiring a capable advertising agency to prepare and place campaign advertisements, reserve television and radio time, prepare brochures, and handle other phases of campaign communications.

If a particular campaign is in a congressional district or smaller unit, it may or may not require an agency—but it is wise to explore the possibilities and the cost before ruling an agency out.

When selecting an agency, the campaign director looks for these things:

Political awareness. Political advertising sometimes is quite different from ordinary advertising, and it would be highly desirable to retain an agency with political background and experience.

Strong art development. One of the chief advantages of having an agency prepare material is the quality of layout and design one can receive from an agency's art department.

Quick service. Political advertisements and literature often must be put together quickly. The agency should be prepared to work nights and weekends to provide the service needed.

Respect within the industry. Most political advertisements are payable in advance but if an agency has the respect of newspapers, radio stations and television stations it can reserve time and space more easily, and delay payment until a more convenient moment.

Adequate personnel. If an agency is small and lacks sufficient personnel to handle several projects simultaneously, it may have trouble filling multiple urgent demands.

No one should expect an advertising agency to run a campaign—and, indeed, no one should want an agency to do so. Here are some things an agency should do:

Reserve radio and television time.

Prepare copy and supervise production of radio and television spots.

Working from suggestions, prepare copy and layouts for campaign literature.

Make layouts for signs, bumper stickers, billboards, posters.

Design campaign stationery, envelopes, and similar materials.

Suggest color combinations, design, etc.

Reserve billboard space; make arrangements for producing and mounting billboards.

Put rough ideas for advertisements and campaign literature into polished final form.

The agency should NOT be expected to:

Determine campaign policy and strategy.

Serve as research arm.

Fulfill the functions of press secretary.

Set up campaign schedules.

Handle mailing and distribution of literature.

Advertising agencies earn the bulk of their income on commissions they receive from placing ads. In a short, intensive campaign they probably will charge an additional base fee, plus production costs on material they prepare.

Indeed, a publicity chairman (with or without a committee), assisted by an advertising agency, can accomplish a great deal. This is especially true if the publicity chairman (called press secretary above) has had professional experience. Even if you have little money for a campaign, endeavor to obtain professional advice on publicity matters. As with surveys and polling, this is no place for an amateur.

Finally, it is important that the public relations specialists be consulted on all aspects of the campaign concerning which they might be able to make useful suggestions. But this does not mean that they should direct everything. This advice runs counter to the policies of some public relations firms, who sometimes insist that, if they are to take over a campaign, they must have the complete say-so. Therefore, on occasion, a candidate and his manager may have a difficult decision to make concerning the relative authority of themselves as opposed to that of some public relations firm. Sometimes the solution lies in a carefully designed agreement with such a firm before they begin work.

2. NEWS, ADVERTISING, AND LITERATURE

For the most part this section deals with printed or published materials, nearly all of which may be distributed in various ways. First, there is *news*. Here are some suggestions about handling this type of publicity from the "official" *Publicity Manual* of the Republican National Committee. This was used in 1964 and is based on a similar item prepared by the Republican State Committee of Massachusetts. It contains the essentials. What is reproduced here assumes that you know how to write a news story in the first place. If not, go to the original document for some suggestions or see the *Campaign Communications Handbook* used by the Democratic National Committee in the same election. Better yet, consult a practicing journalist.

The Groundwork

As publicity chairman for your GOP organization, you'll find that most newspaper editors will depend on you to keep them supplied with news about local Republicans and GOP events. So to lay the groundwork for your publicity campaign, and *before* you write a line of a press release:

1. Learn about each newspaper serving your area.
2. Read each paper thoroughly. Get to know its style. When your news release is written in the style of the paper you're sending it to, the chances are better you'll see it in print.
3. Introduce yourself to the newspaper people you'll be working with, especially any local correspondents ("stringers," in newspaper talk) for large papers. Ask

how you can best work with them. The personal contact is invaluable, and you may meet a few more Republicans.

4.   Learn the deadlines. By what day (if it's a weekly) does the paper want the story? Or, if it's a daily, what time? Then get your story in before the deadline. If it isn't, it won't be used. Most weeklies publish on Thursdays; a few publish Fridays, so it's best to get stories to the editors by Tuesday, because weeklies aren't mechanically geared to immediate publication. For daily newspapers, have your story in the city room 24 hours ahead of the scheduled release date and time. Sunday papers want some stories no later than the preceding Wednesday.

What Kind of News?

Everything your Republican organization does is news. No matter how small or unimportant the event, it warrants at least *two* news releases: one saying it's going to take place and one reporting what happened. If the chairman, secretary and treasurer of your group are going to meet at the chairman's home to talk about the campaign informally, that's an item for the paper—not a big one, but so what? *Constant* publicity is more effective than occasional big splashes. These are news, for instance.

1.   *Every* meeting of two or more persons—before and after.

2.   The local group will do something—and another item when it's done.

3.   The local chairman (or anybody) is going to confer with somebody somewhere else.

4.   Volunteers are needed for something—and another item when they sign up.

5.   Somebody makes a statement, or replies to one.

That's the idea, and it boils down to this: *Every mention of Republican activity is of value.*

One Event, Lots of Publicity

Suppose your Republican committee is planning a dinner with a speaker. That *single* event can result in as many as *eight* different stories in the newspaper. The trick is to start your publicity early. Avoid the one massive story detailing all the plans—a story which the editor may well trim into a piece half the length you've submitted.

Instead, write a series of shorter stories to be released on different days. Then submit them one at a time.

From the single dinner event, you can publicize:

1. Announcement of dinner, with name of chairman.
2. Main speaker named.
3. Appointment of toastmaster.
4. Plans for dinner, with names of other chairmen and committee members.
5. Picture and biography of speaker.
6. Reminder story of dinner.
7. "Dinner to be held tonight" story, recapping plans.
8. Follow-up story (which the editor may want telephoned to him directly after the dinner).

Of course, it has to be a pretty big event to get that kind of a play. But often you can get three, four or more stories out of it.

Working with the Press

Nearly all daily, weekly and Sunday newspapers have certain ground rules, and by sticking with them, you and your stories will be better off.

1. Be the *only* news source for your local Republican organization. Your name on GOP news release paper then will become familiar quickly.

2. Never use pressure or influence to try to get a story printed.

3. Always treat members of competing papers equally. Don't play favorites. The editors will respect your fairness.

4. Cooperate fully with reporters. If one asks you for details on a story, answer his questions without beating around the bush. If you don't know the answers, find them out and call him back.

5. Don't be forever talking to reporters "off the record." If you don't want something published, don't tell it.

6. It's fine to congratulate a reporter on a good story but don't thank him for it. It's the paper's job to print news because it's news, not as a favor to you.

7. Never complain to a reporter or editor that your story didn't appear. The editor isn't "against you" or "anti-Republican." The chances are there was more pressing news that day.

Timing Your News Releases

Most of the time you'll be dealing with "hard news" —stories which need immediate attention. Feature stories usually can be published this week or next and still be timely. But an event occurring today must be reported today, either by telephoning the story to the editor or by writing it and having it delivered overnight. With a daily, *two days later is too late.*

. . . . . .

Photos

Newspapers are always hunting for good pictures to help tell the story and to give the paper more eye appeal. If your local GOP organization is planning an event with good photo possibilities, call and suggest it to the editor. He may send a staff photographer, or may ask you to get him photos. But call him well before the event, not five minutes ahead of time.

. . . . . .

Radio and Television

In your publicity efforts, don't overlook radio and television news directors. They, too, search for local news and when you've got some, they want it. The men to know at your local radio/TV station are the News Director (for news releases) and the Program Director (if you see a chance to get a local GOPersonality on a program).

The prime difference between newspaper and broadcast publicity is that releases for radio and TV should be prepared to be spoken instead of read, so difficult names should be spelled correctly *and* phonetically. While TV prefers film, stills may be used and it's worth it to send a print with the news story.

. . . . . .

When the Press Covers the Event

When an important meeting or other special event is coming up—one which might deserve press coverage—invite the press well in advance.

About a week ahead, mail (or better yet, hand deliver) a written memo to city editors and radio/TV news directors. In it, briefly describe the coming event. What's going to happen? Who's going to speak? Will there be good photo possibilities? Tell the press the bare-bone facts. And be sure to mark it "MEMORANDUM" so the editor will know it's not a release.

Then give the day and date, the time, the place and its address. Finally, include your name, address and phone number.

A few days before the event, follow up with a phone call to city editors and radio/TV news directors as a reminder.

If admission is being charged to the event, never ask newsmen or photographers to pay. They are your guests. Be fully prepared for them and ready to cooperate with them.

In advance of the event you should

1. Obtain from the main speaker a copy of the speech he will deliver, and make copies—or prepare a page of excerpts covering the most important points in the speech.

2. Prepare brief biographical or identifying data about the speaker or honored guest.

3. Prepare a list of other invited guests or head table guests.

4. Provide a list of the officers in your organization.

5. Write a "cover story" about the meeting. The story should be written in straightforward news style, in past tense, and should include the highlights of the meeting and speech.

6. Be sure you have more than enough copies of each data sheet or story for any reporters who might cover the story.

7. Shortly beforehand, set up a press table equipped with all the prepared material, plus extra pencils and paper. Arrange for one of your committee members to staff it.

When the Press Arrives

Reporters are attending your event because it's their job to report the news. Have everything ready. Have someone at the door to meet newsmen and direct them to the press table you've set up. Show them what's available to them, and invite them to meet people they can interview for stories. Answer their questions without hedging. The cooperation you and your associates show to the press and the information you give will pay off in good will and stories.

The next major, and related, problem is *advertising*. Here you will be using many of the news media involved above, but more on your own terms. This time you will be paying for the services; hence you can call the tune.

It is not possible to discuss all the alternatives here. This is what you go to an advertising agency for. See the prior section of this chapter for what to expect from advertising counsel. But here is a brief outline of some things the beginner, especially, needs to know. This is taken from the *Manual of Practical Political Action*, referred to earlier.

Advertising

INTRODUCTION

Political advertising has one important resemblance to commercial advertising. Unless you remember that resemblance, you will lose the effectiveness of your political effort.

In political advertising, as in commercial advertising, you are selling a product. That product has an entity, it has an appeal, and there must be a market either consciously or unconsciously desiring it.

In the case of commercial products, your market consists of potential buyers. In the case of political advertising, your market consists of potential voters, or—in the case of issues—supporters.

WHAT'S YOUR PRODUCT?

In political advertising, your product can be any one of three things. It can be an organization for which you are trying to arouse sympathy and/or membership. For instance, you might be trying to establish a new local political action committee. Your product might be an issue for which you are trying to gain interest and support. For example, the Bretton Woods plan, . . . And finally, your product may be a candidate.

When the product is an organization, advertising usually resembles what is known in the commercial world as institutional advertising This kind of advertising requires long and thorough copy. You seldom can persuade an individual to join a new group by using a catch phrase. Generally, you need painstaking and fully developed argument. For that reason such advertising is usually limited to newspapers, to local magazines, and to direct mail.

When your product is an issue your copy may be brief and argumentative if the issue is already familiar to the public. It is not necessary to develop a long argument to persuade people to engage in a buyer's strike against inflation. All you need do is remind people that prices are going up and urge them to combat this price trend by staying out of the market place. Sometimes the opposition develops the arguments on its side so thoroughly that the public is well aware of the issue. With a few brief words you may be able to reply and here again, small space and brief radio time is usable. If, however, the issue is little understood, if neither your side nor the opposition is developing the arguments, then your issue must be sold in full-length terms, and media offering large space are essential.

INTRODUCING MR. CANDIDATE

When your product is a candidate, the analogy to commercial advertising is very useful. It can be said of any commercial product that it passes through three advertising stages. The first is the introductory, in which the new product is introduced to the market. The second is the competitive, in which you ask support of your product in preference to that of the other fellow's. The third is the reminder stage in which your product has become thoroughly established and your only problem is to keep reiterating its name.

The application of these three stages to a candidate is obvious. . . .

Decisions on the preparation of *campaign literature* and miscellaneous printed materials for distribution to the voters or to various kinds of agencies for display purposes are often difficult. The possibilities are almost endless. They include leaflets, handbills, small cards, photo stories, comic books, tabloid newspapers, postcards and other forms of direct mailing, posters and other display materials, and novelties of all kinds.

Again, consult with your advertising counsel on alternatives. However, on the utility of one kind of literature—the leaflet —at the local level all are agreed. Leaflets serve innumerable purposes. They can help introduce a candidate at a meeting. They are essential when canvassing voters house-to-house. They are usable in direct mailings.

The Democratic National Committee has recently advised the following in its *Campaign Communications Handbook:*

Print at Least One Basic Leaflet

A leaflet provides all the essential information about the candidate in short and comprehensive terms. It is designed to be retained and studied or handed on from one person to another.

A leaflet is not a handbill or "throwaway." It is therefore worth while to spend a little more money on your basic leaflet—print it on heavy paper, perhaps use an extra color, use dignified type. Economize on handbills, but not on leaflets.

A two or three page leaflet (having one or two folds) should fit into a regular business envelope (No. 10)— measuring about 9 1/2 by 4 1/8 inches. In this size, it can be enclosed with letters, mailed by itself, given in

quantities to individuals or groups to distribute with
their own literature, and carried by the voter in a pocket
or purse.

There is also one legal matter which you must not forget
in the preparation of your campaign literature. This is the
fact that in many areas it is a crime to issue political literature
without indicating the name of the sponsor. You must often
label where your printed matter comes from; and this means
the political organization or candidate, not the print shop.

But this is a minor problem compared to that of *literature
distribution*. Leaflets, broadsides, folders, and the like, are of
no use if they do not reach the people for whom they are
intended. Here are a few suggestions, again from the Democratic *Campaign Communications Handbook*.

How to Distribute Campaign Literature

Door-to-door distribution of campaign literature in
selected city or town precincts may be carried out by
Young Democrats or other groups on a volunteer basis,
or by a paid distribution agency. If you are going to pay
for such distribution, be certain the firm you are dealing
with is reliable.

A reminder: Have volunteers distributing literature at
all meetings, large or small, at rallies, on speaking tours,
on street corners. Have volunteers insert literature in
their personal mail. Make up enough copies for all your
volunteers to distribute. When you send out a letter mailing, enclose some literature to supplement the appeal
of the letter.

Another form of literature distribution is through direct
mailings. For information on this procedure see the Democratic *Handbook*. However, direct mailings have declined in
importance in recent years because of their cost compared to
other approaches. For example, to send your leaflet by first
class mail (the preferable way) to 1,000 voters will cost from
$60 to $70. This compares to radio costs, for example, of $1
to $2 per 1,000 listeners. Nevertheless, direct mailings can be

pinpointed better than most other approaches and, for this reason, still have considerable utility if your budget will permit.

3. RADIO AND TV

Though eclipsed by TV in recent years, *radio* is still a major campaign medium. It provides the best way to reach women voters, and, per thousand persons reached, it is cheaper than TV, newspaper advertising, and most forms of literature distribution.

You may broadcast live or by means of recordings. The latter are recommended. See your advertising counsel or the manager of the local radio station for advice on how to produce recorded materials, known as "electrical transcriptions."

The presentations may be in the form of either spot announcements or programs. Most prefer the former. Such "spots" are usually broadcast between programs and take from as much as a minute to as little as 20 seconds. The Democratic *Campaign Communications Handbook* advises that "a one-minute spot announcement should be no longer than 150 words. A 20-second spot should not exceed 55 words." Their suggestions on "spot" preparation follow.

How to write a Spot Announcement

Take great pains in writing your spot announcements. The following rules, though not binding, may help.

1. The opening sentence. Spend time on this. The opening sentence should be interesting, it should be informative, and it should lead into the next sentence. It should be short and simple. And steer clear of questions in the opening sentence, i.e., don't begin "Are you in favor of Federal aid to education?" Some viewers are likely to say "no" and turn the dial.

2. In the body of your announcement, remember that you have no pictures to help carry the thought. Therefore, be very clear, never exceed the word limits listed above, and keep your announcements on *one* subject.

You may introduce sub-points to back up your argument, but you won't have time, even in one-minute announcements, to outline your entire platform.

3. In closing your announcement, be sure to tell the voter to vote for your candidacy. Without such an ending your announcement is wasted.

The same *Handbook* has an excellent summary of what is involved in radio programs. Again, however, to use programs effectively you need the advice and assistance of professionals, either from your advertising agency or the station itself.

Radio Programs

Programs are available in four different lengths: 5 minutes, 10 minutes, 15 minutes, and 30 minutes.

Programs are also available in one-hour lengths, but we strongly advise against long programs. 5-minute and 15-minute periods are long enough to give the listening audience an impression of the candidate and to get across the major campaign ideas.

How to make your programs interesting and attention-getting. A group of radio programs over the course of your campaign should be viewed as a series. Each program should be linked with every other program. Each of the programs should have a distinct subject, although the summary at the end may review each time the total story the candidate wishes to tell. By linking the programs through a theme, and avoiding repetition, the candidate may build a continuing audience that will not only vote for him, but will tell other people to listen and look and to vote the same way.

Your series of programs need not, and in fact should not, consist of straight talks, for it is difficult to hold an audience with a straight talk, no matter how interesting the speaker's remarks are and no matter how pleasing his voice.

Here are a few ways to vary the form of presentation of radio programs:

Be interviewed by a friendly reporter.

Answer questions by a panel of questioners, each member of the panel representing a different voting group, such as a workman, a farmer, a housewife, a home owner, a young person, and so on.

Report to the people. If the candidate is an incumbent in Washington, a series of reports on the actions of Congress and the Administration is an effective theme for several programs.

"On the spot" interviews. If the candidate is a new one, and relatively unknown, consider using transcribed programs made by means of a portable tape recorder in which are presented "on the spot" interviews with a farmer on his farm, for example. Let the farm sounds come through—the tractor engine running, the cows mooing, etc. You might set up other interviews with factory workers, at a public power project, or at an army base. Your local radio station can probably help you arrange for the necessary portable recording equipment.

In characterizing radio as a political medium the Republican National Committee concludes its 1964 discussion of *Radio as a Political Instrument* with the following.

To Summarize

1. Radio coverage reaches many people who don't watch much television.
2. Radio's lower cost and the distinctive character of some radio stations' programming offer the user more of a "rifle" and less of a "shotgun."
3. Local listening habits vary.
4. Voice quality is a vital consideration.
5. Material presented via radio must be in simple terms.
6. Keep repeating the candidate's name.
7. Call for a "saturation" schedule if the opponent is caught off base.

If you have mastered some of the techniques of platform and radio speaking, you should not have much trouble with *television.* In many ways it is a combination of both. The individual performer will find the Republican National Committee's candidate's *Primer on How to Utilize Radio and*

Television Effectively, published a few years ago, an excellent guide. Or, again, consult either your advertising counsel or the TV station concerning dress, notes, lighting, rehearsal, and so on. Television involves a great many technical problems, and it is several times more expensive than radio—about $5 per 1,000 viewers. Therefore it is almost a *must* that you obtain qualified and expert help for a television performance.

Like radio, television uses spots or programs, live or recorded. The principles involved in choosing the alternatives are the same as for radio. It is mainly in the use of visual material that television differs from its predecessor and competitor. The following from the Democratic *Campaign Communications Handbook* will give you some idea of what is involved here.

Your Television Material

In the early days of television most candidates used the medium to present traditional types of speeches. Visual material, if any, was used simply to illustrate the speaker's text, much as a book is illustrated.

Today, however, the best political writers prepare integrated programs, in which the visual material and the text work together for maximum effect. For example, in designing a program the writer will make a list of points the candidate wants to get across, and at the same time he will list visual material which will sharpen or dramatize those points. In other words, "visuals" should be used to heighten meaning, not just to break up monotony.

Visual Aids Are Valuable Aids

Charts, film clips and slides are good tools to sharpen your points. For example, if you are saying that employment has dropped under Republican rule in your area, *show* the voter graphically with a simple, boldly drawn bar chart. Another useful type of "visual" is the mounted newspaper clipping. By showing the voter an actual headline about rising unemployment you not only sharpen your point but add credibility to what you say.

Incidentally, all charts should be drawn on light gray dull finish drawing board, and clippings should be mounted on the same material. If you use still photographs, be sure they are matte finish which will not reflect light, or spray glossies to kill glare.

Check with your local television station to find what types of material it is equipped to handle. In most cases, the station can help you obtain or create "visuals."

Film clips are available from newsreel companies, your local TV station's library, and companies that sell stock footage. Or you can get a local cameraman to take specific shots.

Be careful not to overdo things. Remember that your most important "visual" is the candidate himself. You are trying not only to transfer his ideas into the voter's mind but also to project his personality into the public heart. Too many visual inserts in a program can make it "busy" and weaken the impact of the candidate's appearance.

A limited amount of visual material is available through the Democratic National Committee, 1730 K Street, N.W., Washington 6, D.C. They will be glad to supply this at a nominal charge, and to advise you where you can obtain other material.

VIDEOTAPE

This is to the eye what sound tape is to the ear. The image is recorded magnetically, can be played back immediately, can be erased, and can be edited to insert special "visuals." Generally speaking, the visual quality of a videotape program is better than that of film.

TV stations in all major markets of the U.S. are equipped with videotape equipment, so the chances are good that you can use this technique in preparing your programs.

If not, you always can make your own films.

As for purchasing television time, there are some tricks to the trade. Your advertising counsel will know them, but on the following from the Democratic *Handbook* you should be forewarned:

Where To Buy

Contact your local television stations. They will supply you with coverage maps that indicate the exact area and families they reach. Pinpoint the audience you want to reach and then buy television time that will cover them.

Television Time Costs

Most television stations have local as well as national rates, but some have only one rate—the national rate. When you see the sales managers or salesmen of your local television stations, ask whether there is a local as well as a national rate and, if there is, pay no more than the local rate. This is much lower than the national rate and is the rate paid by local merchants for their advertising. *You should not pay more* than any retail store in your community.

National rates are those paid by the advertiser with national distribution of his product. The Democratic National Committee pays national rates. You must get local rates wherever they exist.

Equal Time

The regulations governing broadcasting make it possible for you to secure as good time as the opposition. So be sure you inquire as to the time periods purchased by the opposition before deciding what time periods you will buy. The Government regulation says that if a station sells time to one political party, it must make available "equal opportunity" to the other party. In other words, you do not need to take "any" time period the station wishes to give you. You can insist on a time period of equal value in terms of advantageous hour and assured audience. The station must obey the Government rules in order to retain its license.

You should know also that, by law, you can not be charged premium rates for television time devoted to politics. Since 1952, political broadcast costs "shall not exceed the charges made for comparable use of such station for other uses."

The Republican National Committee's 1964 pamphlet on *How to Use TV in a Political Compaign* concludes as follows:

To Sum Up

1. Buy the best stations and times in every city. And make the stations show you the audience ratings so that you know what you are getting.

2. Find the vital issues and stick to them. Make them your issues.

3. Dominate the air at the close of the campaign.

4. Beware of long programs; it is hard to get your money's worth out of them. Do strive for a press build-up if you have any.

5. Beware of appearances under circumstances which you cannot control.

6. Always show your candidate at his very best and with as much visual interest as possible.

4. RALLIES, MEETINGS, AND ENTERTAINMENT

As suggested earlier, these public relations devices may require a special chairman as well as committee. The typical advertising agency personnel and public relations counsel may have had little or no experience with political meetings. Therefore, you may wish to have a speakers chairman or meeting chairman or both. A job description which combines the two is contained in the Democratic National Committee's *Guidebook for County and Precinct Workers.*

The Speakers Chairman's Job

The message of the Democratic Party is carried to every corner of the county through this official and his committee. Victory often depends on having enough good local speakers. Candidates, party leaders, community leaders can be enlisted. New speakers and panel leaders can be developed through regular training sessions. Arrangements for national speakers are made through the speakers bureau of the Democratic National Committee in cooperation with the state organization.

Speakers chairmen and their committees have the following responsibilities (sometimes in cooperation with other committees):

1. Stage Democratic rallies and panel discussions.

2. Set up series of small neighborhood meetings, morning coffee hours, afternoon teas, evening get-togethers, where the candidates and party leaders can speak to the voters individually.

3. Place speakers on the programs of nonpolitical, nonpartisan groups in order to reach independent voters. (If you find that a speaker is presenting the opposition's case before such groups, request time to present yours.)

4. Organize speakers' caravans to go into suburbs, small towns, and rural areas.

5. Provide speakers and panel discussion members for radio and television time the publicity chairman may obtain.

6. Train new speakers.

The possibilities here defy full description. Nevertheless, let us consider a few of the most important alternatives.

The general tendency today seems to be to discount the utility of the *mass political rally* as a very effective means of political conversion, when taken by itself. Such meetings are, however, still considered desirable, but more for what may be called their "side effects" than for their immediate influence. That is, mass meetings, if properly handled, may result in large quantities of favorable publicity (free—and this is important) in the press. They will stimulate talk about the candidate, bolster the morale of workers, and perhaps frighten the opposition.

Party conventions, for instance, not only serve to nominate candidates and to provide a party policy, but they also are public relations devices. In their latter role, they should be thought of as simply a special kind of mass meeting, subject to the same problems and same techniques.

But the mass meeting and mass rally need expert guidance. If you want to plan something of this kind, you had better consult someone who has had a good deal of experience. However, an excellent bird's-eye view of the hazards as well as the opportunities involved can be obtained by a quick reading of the "Come One Come All" section of Harold's Gauer's penetrating little book, *How to Win in Politics.*

The other principal kind of political meeting is best typified by the relatively impromptu *streetcorner meeting* involving what is known in large sections of the country as "stump-speaking." This technique may be used without some of the complicated organization and planning which is demanded by the large rally, and, with a little variation, it can be used in the cities as well as in the more rural areas.

Stump-speaking involves the small informal gathering which listens to a more or less impromptu talk by someone traveling through the town or area. The speaker is apt to use a public address system, the equipment for which he carries around with him in his auto. This technique is a "must" in large sections of the Middle West, West, and South. In a modified form, it is frequently used in the cities also.

Here is a vivid description of the problems of a stump-speaker as described in an article specially written for this book by one of the author's former students, Joe Bodovitz, who has had a good deal of experience in this sort of work.

Howdy!
A STUDY OF THE STUMP-SPEAKER IN A POLITICAL CAMPAIGN

Suppose you are the campaign manager of a candidate for statewide office in Oklahoma. You are faced with many problems and decisions, but your most important one is this: what type of campaign will yield the best results, and what is the most effective way to spend campaign funds? This is not an easy question, but on the answer may depend the success or failure of your candidate.

After considering the many factors involved, you may finally decide to use primarily stump-speakers; you will put your candidate on the road as soon as possible, but you will also equip other speakers and send them out to campaign.

These stump-speakers will be college students, or perhaps aspiring young politicians just out of college. They will be sent out to meet people, to shake hands, to talk to crowds wherever they can find them, and to use every means possible to build up good will and support for your candidate. They will be, in short, traveling representatives who combine advertising, personal contact, and public speaking in their attempts to win votes.

If you make this decision, you must make two assumptions first. One of these is that personal contact changes more minds than does influence from far-off or impersonal advertising, although these may be helpful. And you must also have enough money to support stump-speakers, for it can become an expensive process. For you must provide your speakers (usually in teams of two) with a car, a public address system, and plenty of money for gas and oil, living expenses, and salary.

The speaking procedure is this: first, the car is parked in a conspicuous place where the speech is to be made; the amplifiers are turned so that as much area as possible will be covered. The microphone is set up on the sidewalk and plugged in; then a few cowboy records are played loudly. They must be fast, rhythmic songs, usually three or four of them; one of the team announces between each record that the "speakin'" will begin in just a few more minutes. When a fairly large crowd has assembled, he will introduce his partner, who then gives the speech. The introduction is not always necessary; often the same speaker does all the talking.

Judging the crowd is important; a speaker looks foolish standing on a sidewalk talking when there is nobody listening. Unless there are fifteen or twenty people close enough to be obviously interested in the speech, it is usually best to merely shake hands, and not try a speech. This number excludes small children, of whom there are usually fifteen or twenty assembled the minute the car is parked.

If the amplifiers are good, people for some distance around will be able to hear the speech, but it is important not to make anybody mad by being too loud.

In some places it is against city ordinances to use a loudspeaker within city limits; this is always a problem but can usually be solved. Often it is several minutes be-

fore the constable arrives to inform the speaker of the law,
and by this time he has often said all he intended to. Or
the constable may be a supporter of the candidate, and
either purposely waits a few minutes or allows the speaker
to finish a short speech. In most cases, therefore, it is possible to appear very law-abiding and still say as much as
you wanted to say.

After the speech has been made, the speaker plays a
loud march, or preferably "Oklahoma," and a few more
cowboy records while the crowd is breaking up. He immediately starts shaking hands, and listening to all who
wish to talk to him; this group usually includes all the
old-age pensioners in the town, who sit on the sidewalk
all day and are overjoyed to find somebody who virtually
has to listen to them. When there is no particular hurry,
it may be profitable to stay and talk, but on Saturdays,
or whenever there are more speeches to be made, it is
necessary to leave for the next town.

In a week this usually means driving between 1,000 and
1,500 miles. On Oklahoma roads this is hard on the car
and the expense account, but is the only way to cover a
county thoroughly.

So much for the mechanics; what does a stump-speaker
say? This of course depends on the particular campaign.
Some political campaigns are clean, and some are dirty;
the speeches vary accordingly. In the campaign two years
ago, we had clear instructions to talk only about our
candidate, and never to refer to any others. We discussed
his constructive program, which contained, principally,
increased soil and water conservation; this is a vital need
in agricultural areas, but is hardly an issue, since nobody
can oppose it.

Some campaigns are dirty. In one, I often devoted two
thirds of a speech to the unbelievable defects and vices of
other candidates, so that mine was almost an angel when I
finally got around to praising him.

The campaign speech contains as many jokes and stories
as possible; issues are simplified, and the audience is always
urged to vote. This is the basic structure of the speech; it
is broadened or cut down depending on the amount of
time available. Some speeches can be only five or ten min-

utes long; other times, speeches of a half an hour or an hour are required.

The first words of a campaign speech are exceedingly important, for they may well determine whether or not the audience will remain for the rest of the speech. Most speeches usually open with a joke or story, and finding the right one for a rural area is not easy. I have tried many, and the only successful one I have discovered is this: "Just a few minutes ago I was talkin' to a farmer up the road a piece, and he told me that he had been farmin' around here for a long time; he allowed as how he had seen all kinds of ticks—brown ticks, gray ticks, spotted ticks, and a lot more, but that poli-ticks were the darndest ticks he'd ever seen. And that's what I want to talk to you about this afternoon—poli-ticks." After a joke like this, I have never figured out why the people stay, but they do, and a more intelligent story is completely useless.

Is stump-speaking successful? Emphatically, yes. For the stump-speaker, no place is too small to visit, no favor too small to do. He speaks at small towns that no candidates at all will visit, and where no speakers for other candidates will appear. He provides a friendly approach often lacking in politics outside the big-city machines. I once drove for an hour and a half to a tiny community miles from any decent road. It was a hard trip, and it was obvious that no other campaigner would make it. When I finally arrived, I had an audience of 50 or 75 voters. They apparently appreciated the fact that at least one candidate was interested enough in them to personally appeal for their support; my candidate received 85 percent of the votes from that neighborhood.

Another useful version of the stump-speaking or street-meeting technique is known as the *shop-gate rally*. Here is how this works, as described in the United Electrical Workers' *Guide to Political Action*. However, the use of this technique need not be limited to labor unions by any means.

The Shop-Gate Rally

The shop-gate rally is one of the most effective campaign meetings. Such rallies usually take place during the noon lunch period, just outside the gates of large factories. They may be held when shifts are changing and large numbers of workers are either waiting outside the shop gates or are leaving the plant.

It is poor judgment to hold shop-gate rallies exclusively for the out-going shift because most workers are eager to get home and may not stop to listen. The well-timed shop-gate rally is listened to attentively by most workers. The rally can be started by playing music, broadcast over a public address system by means of phonograph records.

The local union should arrange for a shop worker, possibly the Local president, to introduce the main speaker. Introductions should be brief. The main speaker should stand, if possible, in plain view of the workers. Frequently this will be the only chance that hundreds of workers will have of actually seeing the candidate for whom they plan to vote.

With an auto or sound truck, a speaker can sometimes cover a large number of shops during the course of a day. To help do this, schedules of the various lunch hours of important shops should be drawn up ahead of time.

After an enthusiastic shop-gate rally by a candidate, it is usually possible to give large quantities of leaflets and other campaign material to the listening workers who will want to distribute it to other workers in the shop.

Moving on, we come to *caravans* and *parades*.

The old-style torchlight parade is a thing of the past, but it is still not unusual to have a kind of parade just before a large meeting. This helps to gather crowds and to lead them on into the meeting. Like the meeting itself, it provides a dramatic background for obtaining a great quantity of free publicity. However, it also needs to be carefully managed, for a parade easily becomes a very sloppy affair.

The caravan, however, is still a kind of technique which is widely used—especially in the more rural areas, though to some extent in more heavily populated centers. This is how the South Dakota Republican State Central Committee describes the function of the *county caravan* in one edition of its *County Workers' Campaign Manual.*

The Country Caravan

MAKE IT PEPPY!

Many counties have had great success in securing additional votes for *all* of their Republican candidates by conducting at least one countywide political caravan scheduled to visit every town and city in the county. All county candidates should participate in this caravan with each driving a separate car if possible and with each helping to hand out personal campaign cards, party literature, circulars, etc. Caravans should be *run on schedule;* they should be publicized in all county papers in advance showing just when the caravan will visit each community; if possible a small band or a loud speaker system carrying records and having a microphone for use in street corner speeches should be taken with the caravan. Make the stops short, snappy, and full of pep. Have the candidates mingle in the crowds, visit the people in the stores and shops, placard the community with literature. Usually caravans are held on the day of a big G.O.P. evening rally at some central point. Advertise that rally; invite all to attend it—make each caravan stop cheerful, snappy, and friendly. Give a couple of short, peppy speeches over your amplifying system and *keep moving according to schedule.*

It should not be forgotten that the caravan is a money-saving device as well as an effective political mechanism.

There are, however, a number of other kinds of political meetings of a miscellaneous sort. It is impossible to describe them all, but two more quotes from the South Dakota *County Workers' Campaign Manual* will illustrate some of the things that can be done.

The County Republican Picnic

BRASS BANDS; ICE CREAM; BUNTING; SHORT TALKS!

Many counties either hold separate county Republican picnics or join with neighboring counties to hold bicounty or tricounty G.O.P. picnics. Invite some prominent, effective, peppy outside speaker—introduce all county candidates present—give free coffee, ice cream, and lemonade and urge families to come and bring their picnic dinners. If possible, invite in a band. Put up some red, white, and blue bunting; tack up plenty of signs and placards. Arrange to move indoors at some nearby point if it rains. These picnics are ideal places at which candidates can get on a first-name basis with many of the voters. Keep them informal and lively—don't let the programs get too long. Day County always holds a four-county "kick-off picnic" to start the campaign; Lake, Moody, Brookings, and Kingsbury Counties usually hold a four-county picnic at Lake Madison, Lake Herman, or Lake Campbell. Invite everybody to attend!

The Precinct Party

COFFEE CAKE DISCUSSION

Frequently small, informal precinct coffee parties, or women's teas held in the home of some good Republican family or in a rural school house or church basement, are among the *most effective* political rallies of a campaign. Remember *voters* are usualy won over one at a time— many times it is easier to win them over at a small, friendly, intimate informal meeting than at a major rally. Literature can be distributed at these small meetings; questions can be asked and answered; county candidates should be invited to attend and should be introduced around. Sometimes one of the local ladies or gentlemen—perhaps the hostess, perhaps one of the county candidates—makes a short, informal speech on the campaign issues with emphasis on the character of the Republican program and personalities. Some of our more active and successful counties arrange for at least *one precinct party* in every precinct of the county during the campaign—especially in *all rural precincts*. This is a specific job for precinct committeemen and women to undertake. Almost every precinct has some large and friendly home whose owners will be glad to have the party in it and several friendly neighbors can "chip in" to provide the coffee, cake, and sandwiches.

You should also make the most of some of the things which

will go farthest to liven up a meeting. These are *plays, skits, fashion shows, music* and other kinds of miscellaneous entertainment.

The use of music and records has already been mentioned as a "must" in stump-speaking. This principle applies equally well to all kinds of meetings. There is no one place to go for information on music for political purposes, but there always are a lot of people in any community who know something about popular music and who enjoy taking part in musical activities.

Here are some of the possibilities: (1) parodies on old songs; (2) current favorites in songs and records; (3) folk songs; (4) street singing and mass singing at rallies; (5) marching songs and music for parades; (6) solos, quartets, and other combinations of local or professional talent; (7) encouragement of clapping and stomping with your music; (8) instrumental music varying from the common banjo to full bands; (9) music over loudspeakers; (10) specially composed music or lyrics or both.

The possibilities are almost endless and few political organizations exploit them to their fullest. As one organization has put it, "there isn't any speech or discussion that can't be enlivened and pointed up by music."

Nor should the use of skits, short dramas, and plays be forgotten. As with music, there is usually someone in the local community who enjoys directing these kinds of activities. He or she, in turn, can make use of the innumerable amateurs who enjoy—or who would like to try their hand at—theatrical work.

Finally, there are the numberless *stunts* and *gimmicks* which can be used for political purposes. These may vary from skywriting to bonus marches, and from song-and-dance acts to hanging someone in effigy. There is no good summary of these possibilities, and the best that was available—in the last section of the NCPAC's *Manual of Practical Political Action* —has been out of print for several years. But you are limited only by your imagination.

5. CONCLUSION

The main point that needs to be emphasized here is that mastery of publicity techniques is not the answer to politics. The secret is in the proper mixture of personality, issues, organization, and technique. If you have nothing to sell, saying it well is probably not going to help you much. But if you do have something worthwhile in mind, a working knowledge of the things discussed in this chapter will help.

Chapter 12

Person-to-Person Activities

Experienced politicians have always believed that personal confrontation of the voter is the most effective way to influence him. As one experienced group has put it: "The effectiveness of a political organization is measured by the extent of its 'in-person' front-door delivery of facts and ideas."

Recent social science studies have done much to confirm this view. Therefore more emphasis has been placed here on this kind of political work—usually called *canvassing*—at the grass roots level than upon any other single form of "selling" technique.

The essence of canvassing is the personal conversation on the prospective voter's doorstep or in his home. But you can also reach more and more people over the telephone, and telephone canvassing is becoming more popular. Finally, there is the all-out type of effort known as the registration or voting drive, which frequently uses almost all types of public relations media in addition to personal contact. All these approaches are discussed here, as follows:

1. *general precinct canvassing*, involving basic procedures which apply across the board;
2. *telephone canvassing* as a specialized technique; and
3. *registration and voting drives*.

To help you interpret some of the canvassing literature, you should know that the kind of work involved here is also often termed "block work," "checking," "interviewing," "polling," "doorbell-ringing," or "taking a census." All these refer to the person-to-person approach in politics.

1. GENERAL PRECINCT CANVASSING

Canvassing is the essence of precinct and block work. In its most complete form, precinct canvassing of the voter aims at: (1) locating prospective voters, (2) identifying their probable political leanings, (3) attempting to influence those on the fence to think your way, and (4) getting people to register and vote. Some nonpartisan registration and voting drives may emphasize steps (1) and (4) exclusively. Even some party organizations do not do much with step (3), relying on radio, TV, and other mass media to do most of the converting. But the best, and most thorough, approach involves all four of these activities.

One of the best general discussions of the canvassing process is contained in the United Electrical Workers' *Guide to Political Action*. Here is part of the chapter on "Canvassing." This discussion also illustrates the importance which labor organizations are now placing on this type of local political work.

Canvassing

Veteran political organizations have learned that nothing can replace a personal visit by a representative of the party organization to the home of the voter. There is no substitute for plain, door-to-door visiting, known as canvassing.

Labor has already learned certain facts about canvassing.

1. Area. People who do door-to-door visiting (canvassing) should not be given too large an area to cover. Canvassers become discouraged if they are assigned many blocks of homes which they cannot visit within a short time. It is much better to give each canvasser a small area and let the job be done thoroughly.

2. Location. Whenever possible, the canvasser should be given an area to canvass which lies within his or her home neighborhood. The closer it is to the canvasser's home, the better. . . .

3. Meeting People. Learning to canvass comes with experience. A good method of showing proper methods of canvassing is to send on experienced person with each new canvasser. People who canvass for the first time may meet with discouragements. . . .

But a canvasser quickly finds that such experiences are the exceptions rather than the rule. The average person visited is hungry for information and a guide to political action today. The canvasser soon learns to state the reason for the visit quickly and clearly. He finds most people he visits friendly and eager to cooperate. As a matter of fact, a canvasser must constantly guard against staying too long in any one home, despite the temptation to do so.

After a period of canvassing, the average person will look forward to meeting with people. He or she will gain confidence. This confidence will come from the realization that there is nothing more important than carrying the message of political action to friends and neighbors.

4. Information. In order to avoid seeming nosy, canvassers should make it clear to each person visited why questions are asked. As soon as the average person understands why his or her visitor is asking the questions, all information asked will be willingly given. *Arguments should be avoided*. Even when the reception is not at first cordial, canvassers should be polite and well mannered. It may require a few visits to win the confidence of some

well-meaning people. But a polite manner of treating all people is the best means of obtaining information and co-operation. Thank the person for answering the questions. Promise to call again. Then be sure you do call again, if you have said you will.

5. Registration. Canvassing campaigns may be organized for many purposes. Perhaps signatures are being collected on a petition. Perhaps people are being asked to attend a mass meeting. Whatever the main purpose, the interview should always include the subject of registration. It is always possible to spend an extra minute inquiring whether all eligible people in the household are registered to vote. If there are unregistered voters, a record of this should be carefully made, just as the canvasser will make a record of registered voters in order to get the vote out on election day.

6. Leaflets. It is useful for canvassers to carry with them several copies of important leaflets issued locally or by the International Office. If there are unregistered people visited, a leaflet should be left explaining why registration is important and how, where, and when to register. The same applies to other campaign issues. Some precinct captains even prefer to distribute leaflets generally in a neighborhood that is to be canvassed. This helps familiarize the people with the subject and saves the canvasser time when personal calls are made.

7. Records. Each canvasser should keep a notebook or record of each family visited. The record should include names, correct addresses, registered and unregistered members of families, party affiliations if any, trade union, phone number if any, whether people in the family are interested in helping with political action work, and any other notes helpful in future relations with the family. On many occasions the canvasser learns of a problem facing a family which political action can help solve. Note of this should be entered on the record. The best time of day or night to visit a person is also a useful piece of information to be entered on the record.

8. Identification. Canvassing should be as systematic as possible. The best results are obtained when the can-

vasser is regularly assigned the same homes to visit. It is even more helpful if visits can be made at regular intervals. Identification cards, pins, or letters should be supplied all canvassers.

Calling cards are a useful device to help the voter remember the canvasser and who he represents. They serve also as a handy and simple means of introduction. Here is an example of such a card along with a few comments about it, as shown in the Republican National Committee's *Workers' Manual*.

Calling Cards

The county committee will find that an investment in calling cards for the precinct workers will pay dividends in votes. The cards should . . . bear the information that the caller is the *Republican* precinct committeeman or woman; that voting information or other assistance will be cheerfully given. The name, address, and telephone number of the *worker* should be printed on the card. A *card* should be left at each house whenever a call is made.

GREETINGS, FELLOW AMERICANS:

I am your neighbor—You and I live in a free country and it is our responsibility to keep it so. It can remain free only so long as the citizens take an interest in their government and vote their convictions.

My job is to answer any question from people in our neighborhood about voting and elections.

Put this card where you can find it and call me anytime I can be of help.

Your Republican Precinct Committee member.

Name_____

Address_____

Telephone No. _____

Figure 6

Also of use will be a small set of 3 x 5 cards, on which you have typed or written out some of the pertinent information that you want to remember to use while you are canvassing.

On one card you will want the record of the candidate ready for quick reference. On other cards you may want to have a few useful facts typed out concerning one or more issues in which your neighborhood is especially interested. Perhaps, for instance, a housing bill is pending in the city council or in Congress. You will want to be able to talk some sense about housing. Pertinent facts and figures can be on your "housing card."

On a few more cards you may want to put down arguments which are useful in replying to some of the points of view which you find expressed in your conversations with voters who may be doubtful about your party's or organization's candidates or issues. These cards are sometimes called "rebuttal cards."

Special problems are often met with in the canvassing of apartment houses in the cities. Many apartment buildings are closed to salesmen, solicitors, and the like. They simply can not get in. In such cases one must work from inside. This means inquiring among your other workers about friends and acquaintances in each apartment building. Develop a list of possible "special contacts" who may be telephoned and asked to assist in the canvassing work. It is rare that you can not find someone in each apartment house—often more than one—sympathetic to your cause and willing to work.

Some suggestions on the use of special contacts are available in the *Campaign Manual* of the Republican National Committee.

Utilizing the Special Contacts

Each special contact may be utilized in several ways:

1. He or she may be willing to do the canvassing in all or part of the building, and become a regular worker of the campaign operation.

2. Such a special contact may be able to recruit other

workers in the building, following the basic policy of decentralization.

3. Special contacts in a single apartment house may, as the campaign progresses, stage meetings, parties, receptions, etc., in the building, at which the candidate and other campaign figures may appear personally and meet the voters and at which enthusiasm may be further developed.

4. Special contracts may be put on the literature distribution drop file, so that an appropriate quantity of each piece of literature may be sent to each special contact for distribution in the building.

5. Special contacts may also arrange for putting campaign posters in the foyer and elevators of the building, and for the posting of notices for registration, voting, rallies, meetings, etc.

6. At the very least, special contacts in an apartment house can always enable a regular canvasser to get in the building and do the canvassing himself.

Of course, while you may be attempting to "convert" someone you are visiting, you are also obtaining information of use to your own organization. *What do you do with this information?*

Good procedure suggests recording certain data for future reference. You can not keep all the information about your voters in your head. And there need to be good records for the person who may succeed you as a precinct worker. Of course, in small local areas where everybody knows everyone else, permanent records about individual voters may be unnecessary. But in populous precincts where there is some turnover in population and where you do not always know your voters personally, records are a must. This is especially true if you expect to make return visits to particular voters and wish to pinpoint your efforts. Moreover, good records permit you to estimate your success, or lack of it, with some precision.

The best approach is to carry with you a small form which can be made out in duplicate at the end of an interview. One copy can remain with the precinct worker, with the other going into a permanent precinct headquarters file. Again, in smaller precincts a single card in one central file may be enough. Use your best judgment.

The following "voter's card" is currently recommended by the Massachusetts Republican State Committee. On the back of the card there is room to show any preferences the voter might have for various kinds of volunteer work at either election time or "year round." This is an extremely complete card which covers a maximum number of possibilities. If you can do with less, by all means devise a simpler form.

```
(Please print with pen)          City/Town _____

                                 Ward _____ Precinct _____

_____        _____  _____
        Voting Name              No.      Street

Occupation _____  Telephone No. _____

Registered  R □  D □  Unenrolled □     Date eligible to register _____

Inclination: R □  D □  None □       Attitude toward visit: Favorable □
                                                           Indifferent □
                                                           Hostile □

Number in home approaching voting age:

Name _____  Name _____

   Date of 21st birthday _____  Date of 21st birthday _____

                                 NEEDS

Absentee Ballot □                    Transportation □
   Serviceman/woman □                    Time _____
   Traveller □
   College student □                 Sitter □
Shut-in: □  at this address □            Time _____
            hospital □
            nursing home □       _____
Just moved from another          Call made by            Date
   city or town □                Information on other side □
```

Figure 7

This kind of card system is becoming more popular. However, in some areas, the use of "polling books" or sheets like the one in Figure 8 is required. The information is first collected on these sheets and then summaries of certain of the data may be compiled at headquarters for other purposes. This can involve a good deal of transposing. This sample poll book page is from a *Precinct Handbook* published by the Democratic National Committee.

Suggested Form for Street Lists

Date Information Obtained __July 15__   By Whom __Harry Smith__

Street __Olive Street__   Ward __12__   Precinct or District __7__

STREET NUMBER & APT. NO.	NAME OF EACH RESIDENT OVER 21	TELEPHONE NUMBER	PARTY PREFERENCE	REGISTERED (YES OR NO)	WHEN LAST VOTED FROM THAT ADDRESS	REMARKS
2300 Block (South Side)						
2360	John Abbott and Mary Abbott	Na 8-1414	Dem.	yes	1962	Needs transportation to polls
	Roger Jones (Lodger)	Em 3-6151	Rep.	yes	1964	
2366	George Bernard Fellspan					
Apt. 1	Ju 6-1212	Ind.	no		1964	Offered to type
	Susan B. Toney	Ti 8-6060	WS	no	1964	Needs baby sitter
Apt. 2	Robert B. Jones	Na 6-1515	Dem.	yes	1962	
2370 (North Side)						
2361	Mr. and Mrs. Raymond Hooper	Ki 6-5656	Dem.	yes	1962	Will provide transportation on election day
2363	George Harris	Sy 8-1540	Ind.	no	1964	
2369	Mary Boswell	Em 6-8080	Rep.	yes	1962	
2400 Block (South Side)						
2460	Mr. and Mrs. James Roberts	Em 8-6600	I. R.	no	1964	Such as: Will he work for Democratic Party? Invalid? Not a citizen? Doesn't want to be called. Works nights—call between hours of 5 and 9 P.M.
	Include persons in military service, hospital patients, students, etc.; who normally reside there.	Roomers or relatives with different family name may have another phone number.	Use letters to indicate party: D—Dem. R—Rep. I—Ind. ID—Ind. Dem. IR—Ind. Rep. FL—Farm Labor WS—Won't Say			

Figure 8

The canvassing or polling record is the basic tool of the political organization. One canvass will go a long way toward indicating how much effort must be put out in any given campaign. But campaigning is not a static affair and voters' minds change. Therefore, the canvassing and polling must be kept as up to date as possible. This is a continuous process and one which cannot be overemphasized. This process also provides one of the very best means of utilizing the efforts of large numbers of volunteer workers, especially women.

2. THE TELEPHONE CANVASS

Another technique which the political parties and others are using increasingly is the *telephone canvass*. It is normally used in addition to, rather than in place of, the efforts of precinct and block workers as described in the preceding section. This technique can be used before election day and for both registration and voting drives as well.

One of the more complete sets of directions for the conduct of a telephone canvass is found in the 1964 edition of the *Democratic Campaign Manual*. A useful abbreviated item is available from the Republican State Committee of Pennsylvania.

The Telephone Campaign

A properly conducted telephone campaign is one of the most effective projects in every campaign.

It is an ideal way to make full use of the time of housewives, elderly persons, and others who want to help out in the campaign but cannot come to headquarters to work. A telephone campaign permits a person to work at his own home, at his own hours and pace, with a minimum of personal inconvenience. (The home effort can, of course, be most effectively supplemented by a bank of telephoning volunteers working at headquarters.)

The telephone committee should be organized on a community or county basis. A dependable volunteer with a fair amount of free time should be placed in charge.

Responsibilities of the telephone chairman include:
Lining up sufficient numbers of workers to make the calls.

Making individual worker assignments, and getting these assignments to the workers.

Preparing instruction sheets and the message to be used in the telephone campaign, and getting these to workers.

Following up on worker assignments to make certain the calls are being made as scheduled.

The goal of the telephone campaign is to contact *every* household in the area to be covered.

Telephone numbers should be transferred to voting lists when possible. In most localities, telephone directories by street are available at nominal cost, which enables this operation to be completed quickly and effectively.

The number of a household should be listed only once; i.e., if there are four registered voters at 100 Main Street, it is necessary to list only one number for this household.

Volunteers should be asked to take a precinct (if lists are available by precinct) or some other list requiring between 300 and 500 calls.

Volunteers should call every voter listed. This system eliminates calls to unregistered voters.

IF THE BASIC METHOD IS NOT FEASIBLE

Telephone calls will be made directly from the local telephone directory. This eliminates the necessity for the task of transferring telephone numbers from directories to voting lists.

Every person in the telephone book should receive a call from a Democratic volunteer. There will be a slight amount of wasted effort here when calls are made to homes which do not contain a registered voter, but this is offset by the saving in time.

Assignments should be made by page number in the telephone directory, with 300 to 500 names assigned to each volunteer. This might be one page in the telephone directory or two or three pages, depending upon the size of the community. A volunteer might be assigned, for example, to call every residence telephone number listed on page 47 of the local telephone directory.

MISCELLANEOUS INSTRUCTIONS TO BE GIVEN TELEPHONE VOLUNTEERS

No calls should be made to business numbers.

Remember—when you are calling for your candidate, you represent him to the people you call. Be polite and courteous. If someone asks you a question about President Johnson or your candidate that you cannot answer, please state that you will be pleased to have a committee member familiar with the subject call back with a detailed reply. (Note the name, number and question for the committee, and the return call will be made by the appropriate committee member.)

If anyone that you call is rude or discourteous, terminate the conversation as quickly as you politely can.

If a child answers, ask for his parents or some older person. If someone answers who does not speak English, is hard of hearing, or for some other reason cannot understand your message, terminate the conversation quickly and politely.

Do not call between _____ P.M. and 7:30 P.M. because this is the time most people have dinner. Do not call before 9 A.M. or after 10 P.M.

If you have any questions, call headquarters.

Note should be made of replies that are unusual, for information of the committee.

Take the names and addresses of persons requesting transportation to the polls and give this information to headquarters.

On election day, if you are not assigned to other campaign work, call in as many names on your lists as you have time. This will remind people to go out to vote.

MESSAGE FOR DEMOCRATIC TELEPHONE VOLUNTEERS

"This is the (name of candidate) for (name of office) Committee calling, asking you to support President Johnson by voting for (name of candidate) for (office).

"May we provide you with transportation to the polls when you go to vote Democratic on Tuesday, November 3.

"Remember—the polls in (name of community) are open from ———— A.M. to ———— P.M.

"Thank you very much."

Note: This is the basic message to be used in all states. It may be necessary to make slight changes in certain states, but the message for volunteers should be substantially the same as above.

Instruction sheets for volunteers and the basic message may be mimeographed in local or district headquarters.

This program will assure complete utilization of women available for campaign "home work."

It provides a simple, direct method of projecting the names of President Johnson and your candidate into the home, thus increasing interest in and discussion of the candidacy.

If conducted during the ideal period of two weeks prior to the election it will serve to alert the voter to the upcoming election.

It is an integral part of our overall program to achieve maximum impact through use of every available campaign techniques.

This is the recommended chronology for telephone campaign:

No later than October 1—Local telephone chairmen appointed.

No later than October 15—Chairmen make specific assignments and distribute telephone kits to volunteers.

No later than October 20—Start making calls.

No later than November 2—Complete all calls.

3. REGISTRATION AND VOTING DRIVES

These efforts consist essentially of a stepped-up canvassing program aimed first at registration and then at getting out the vote. This is usual procedure among the best organized of the party mechanisms. Most of the techniques outlined in the previous section are utilized, but in a completely organized way.

The following arrangement, outlined in the 1964 *Campaign Kit* of the Republican State Executive Committee of Florida, is typical. The intent is that the effort outlined here be undertaken twice—once during the registration period and then again just prior to the election.

1. *Develop a registration calendar and a campaign calendar*
2. *Schedule each target precinct*
   a. Set a definite date (or more than one date for extra-large precincts).
   b. Determine the place where the canvassers will meet.
   c. Set the time for 6:30 P.M.
3. *Prepare the kits of materials for each precinct*
   a. Put enough material for 30 houses in each kit.
   b. Stuff the kits with authorized materials only.
   c. Put the cards in correct order.
   d. Notify precinct chairman where and when materials can be picked up.
4. *Determine how many canvassers are needed for each precinct*
   a. Man-Woman couples are preferable.
   b. Each couple can call on about 30 houses in one evening—20 houses in neighborhoods where houses are far apart.
5. *Assign the correct number of volunteers to each precinct*
   a. Phone them each weekend; determine which evening they will canvass during the following week!
   b. Tell them where to report.
   c. It is helpful to re-call each volunteer one day in advance as a reminder.

EXTRA TIP

In counties where door-to-door canvassing is new, a kick-off meeting of the canvass volunteers is advisable.

The meeting should be used for motivation and training purposes.

6. *Make "advance calls" to each precinct*
   a. See that everything is set (cards and materials picked up).
   b. Review the canvass procedure with the chairman.
   c. Answer any last-minute questions.
7. *Conduct the canvasses on each assigned evening*
   a. Hold the precinct instructional meeting.
   b. Divide into couples.
   c. Give them their materials.
   d. Report back to the meeting place.
   e. Fill out canvass tally sheet.
8. *Report the tally sheet results to headquarters*
   a. How many "for."
   b. How many "against."
   c. How many "not at home."
   d. Send canvassed cards to headquarters for election day preparation.
9. *"Clean-up" canvasses*
   a. Call on "not-at-home" and households that were missed at first canvass.
   b. Try to use known precinct workers without relying on central pool of volunteers being called from headquarters.
   c. Be sure to send cards to headquarters after clean-up canvassing is finished.

A typical Canvass Committee includes:
Canvass Chairman
Scheduling Chairman
Kits and Materials Chairman
Volunteer Recruiting and Assignments Chairman
Advance Calls Chairman
Election Day Chairman

The cards referred to above are similar to the "voter's card" illustrated earlier in this chapter.

Almost any organization—partisan or nonpartisan—can conduct such a door-to-door drive. There are ample training materials available. These vary from the *Democratic Precinct*

Worker's Course of the Democratic National Committee and the AFL-CIO *Register and Vote Manual* to the Republican oriented *Precinct Action Course* prepared by Civic Affairs Associates, Inc. of Washington, D.C. There are special instructor's guides available for both the Democratic and Republican training courses.

Such a drive may be supplemented by a full-scale publicity effort, with the aim of mobilizing the entire community. Here newspapers, radio and TV stations, churches, business leaders, veterans and fraternal groups, trade unions, and the like may all be involved. The possibilities are enormous and can not be dealt with here. However, these are apt to require professional guidance. Illustrative information and materials are available from both national party headquarters as well as from the AFL-CIO Committee on Political Education. See also Chapter 11 here.

4. CONCLUSION

Finally, a *warning*—from the Independent Voters of Illinois' *Manual for Precinct Work*.

> *Remember this:* Although every precinct is different, and although your *particular* precinct may run heavily Democratic or heavily Republican, and although you may have a small precinct or a big precinct—*on the average,* one third of the people will not give you any idea of how they feel about your candidates. Some will slam the door in your face. Some will be polite and say nothing. Some will scold you.
>
> Don't let it worry you—except for this: People who don't talk will usually vote against you. If people tend to agree with you, they'll usually say so. Some will tell you they disagree with you. A very few may agree with you, but not reveal it. But generally, when your precinct list is all marked with plusses, minusses, zeros—you'll find a third are zeros, unknowns. Most likely these votes will turn out to be against you. Beware the temptation to credit yourself with a half or a third of the unknowns. Play safe and credit these to the opposition.

Chapter 13

Election Day
and
After

Usually we think of elections in terms of voting someone into office—from the President of the United States to a
hide and animal inspector. But there are also primaries for
nominations. Moreover, elections can mean the approval of
many things besides individuals.

Constitutions are amended on election day. Initiatives and
referenda are passed upon. Bond issues are approved or dis-
approved. School district mergers are voted in or out. Nor do
elections come around only in the fall of years divisible by
four. "Election day" is really many days.

Whenever election day arrives, there are certain recurring
and typical problems involved. Some of these affect the individual voter who must now play his personal role. Others
primarily concern the special election day preparations of
political parties and governmental agencies.

It is these special preparations which we will consider in this chapter. More specifically, they involve

1. *organizing for election day,*
2. *administering the election,*
3. *guarding against fraud,* and
4. *evaluating the results* as a guide to the future.

Unless these matters are successfully dealt with, all other organizational work is to no avail. The ultimate test lies in the ballot box.

1. ELECTION DAY ORGANIZATION

Election day especially tests the party organizational segment (see Chapter 5) consisting of the special election day committees. Of course, these will have been activated well before election day, and perhaps gradually augmented from the other committees (registration, for example) whose work is largely done. For a suggested timetable for these and related activities, see Chapter 9.

There is general agreement that at least six functions must be handled on election day. At the county level there will be a committee for each function. At the precinct level a single person may work on several functions at various times. General job descriptions for five of the functional committees have been outlined in the *Workers' Manual* of the Republican National Committee.

Committees to be Organized for the Election

CHECKERS COMMITTEE

This committee functions on election day (both primary and general). Its duty is to make sure that every *eligible* voter in the precinct casts his vote. The chairman of the checkers committee must be supplied with a *list* of all persons who will vote the Republican ticket. Telephone numbers are absolutely necessary. The committee will be divided into teams—the number to be determined by the size of the precinct. Each *team* must be given a duplicate list on which to check the voters as their ballots are cast. The teams will take turns at the polling place. As the teams change shifts the one being relieved will report back to headquarters and check the *"Master List."* Then the telephone committee will go into action and start a check with all voters who have not been to the polling place, reminding them of the time the polls close. If it is found that transportation or sitters are required *separate lists* must be made up and given to the chairmen of the transportation and sitters committees. These two committees will then proceed to service the needs. The big *"roundup"* by the checkers committee should occur in midafternoon, thereby allowing *sufficient time* to reach every voter on the Republican precinct list.

TRANSPORTATION COMMITTEE

This committee functions on election day. Drivers should be on hand at the headquarters at all times. The chairman of the transportation committee must have a crew of *well-organized, careful drivers*. The precinct should be divided into sections small enough to give prompt service to the voters who require it. As in the case of the sitters committee, *advance assignments* can be made for transportation from information gathered from the precinct poll.

SITTERS COMMITTEE

Sitters are just what the word implies and are a very important part of the precinct organization. The committee will serve on election day (both primary and general) as sitters in homes where such service is required. The chairman of the sitters committee will select the membership with careful consideration. *Young people* can be used on this committee. The *canvass* of the precinct before the election may reveal specific advance assignments for which arrangements can be made ahead of time. The election day assignments are *"emergency."* The committee, therefore, should be large enough to handle them efficiently.

HEADQUARTERS COMMITTEE

This committee serves in the precinct headquarters during the campaign and on election day. They *assist* the precinct committeeman and woman in all of the details and in the co-ordination of all activities of all committees. They do the clerical work and typing; receive the callers; act as an information bureau; they are the *"jacks of all trades."*

TELEPHONE COMMITTEE

The business of this committee is *telephoning.* The most important function is getting voters to the polls on election day. At intervals during the day *lists* of those who have *not voted* are given to the telephone committee. The chairman will then assign *specific areas* to the members of the committee. It is each person's task to find out why the elector has not voted. If *transportation* is needed, the transportation committee is notified. If a *sitter* is required that committee is notified and goes into action. A committee of substantial numbers will make for efficiency.

During the campaign the telephone committee helps the meetings and radio committees in building audiences. It may assume the responsibility of manning the telephones in the headquarters.

The organization above combines the functions of both polling and checking under the checkers committee. Some would recommend that these two crucial activities be separated. Either way is quite acceptable, depending upon local conditions and the personnel available.

In addition to these committees the Democratic National Headquarters has on occasion recommended a challenge committee. For reasons which will be obvious from the job description below—as outlined in the *Precinct Handbook*—there is a good deal of merit in forming such a committee.

Challenge Committee

Members of a challenge committee operate in the polling place. The number of challengers depends on state laws. Usually they must have credentials. There is ordinarily one for each political party. Challenger's duties are:

1. See that ballot box is empty or machine registers zero before voting starts.

2. Know state laws thoroughly.

3. Challenge anything irregular or against the law, such as a known nonresident voting.

4. Refer to the Election Commission any point which is challenged if it cannot be settled by election officials at the polling place.

5. Watch every vote counted, including absentee.

If you wish to combine checking and challenging in one committee, this is feasible too. However, checking must not be neglected, for in many ways it is the most essential election day activity. Actually, checking is nothing but a last minute form of canvassing, subject to the general rules of canvassing as outlined in the previous chapter.

The general flow of election day activities is suggested by the following from the Democratic National Committee's *Guidebook for Democratic Organization in the County and Precinct.*

The Polls Open

First on the list of election day excitements comes the casting of votes by every Democratic worker. This early voting of all workers in all precincts not only sets a good example, but frees minds for the day's activities. A friendly call from county headquarters to each precinct to check on this starts the day well.

It is an excellent plan to have a Democratic lawyer on duty at the county headquarters. Expert counsel will then be at hand if votes are challenged or after difficulties of this nature occur.

Vote Checkers

Many voters will go to the polls without the assistance or knowledge of precinct workers. Vote checkers, stationed as near voting booths as local custom permits, should check vote casters throughout the day, by party

affiliation when possible, and report names to precinct headquarters at frequent intervals. This is essential to assure that every possible vote is cast.

The County Command

The county chairman and vice-chairman are election day's generals. To them precinct leaders look for advice and help. Decisions must be made promptly. Just as total registration was the goal at the campaign's beginning, so total voting is the goal at campaign's end.

The Polls Close

With the closing of the polls county headquarters becomes the focus of activity. Vote counts begin to come in from polling places. Tallies are kept. Totals may be announced to crowds in the street from a headquarters loud speaker.

Excitement and good will, hopes and fears, will mark these early evening hours.

Whatever the final figures, each Democratic worker will have won a victory of sorts by disciplined action within the framework of the county organization, by the sacrifice of time and energy, by his or her channelled devotion to democracy and the Democratic party.

In any event, whatever the form of your organization for election day, it ought to encompass the process and functions outlined above. For the relationship of temporary election day committees to the more permanent committees, see Chapter 5, which also suggests typical relationships of lower level to high level committees with similar general functions.

2. ADMINISTERING THE ELECTION

Elections do not run themselves. Somebody has to print the ballots, arrange for election supplies, select the election judges and clerks, rent the polling places, arrange for the delivery and servicing of voting machines, count the votes, and announce the results. All this takes a good deal of organization and the time of a lot of people, especially if it is to be well and honestly done.

However, election management is something about which most people know very little. Therefore, this section is oriented toward the role of government officials in the election process. The place and interests of the political parties and other civic organizations will be brought out where their participation is either desirable or legally required.

The general management of a local election is usually in the hands of a board of election commissioners or an election manager of some sort operating under their authority or under the general supervision of a county or city clerk, the county judge, the county auditor or some similar official. This board or agency is responsible for supervising the operation of the election.

Officials are then appointed (elected in a very few cases) to handle individual precincts and polling places. The normal local polling officials are (1) judges, (2) inspectors, (3) clerks, (4) watchers or challengers, (5) a limited number of other political party representatives, and, frequently, (6) a policeman or detective or two.

Judges, inspectors, and clerks actually administer the election and receive special pay, $5 to $25 usually, for their efforts. Normally these persons may not all be from the same political party. In a few places individuals who wish to do this work must pass a preliminary examination. But usually these temporary jobs are open to persons nominated by various members of the political parties and are a part of the normal political patronage. In fact, most parties are extremely interested in getting their own workers appointed to these jobs—for obvious reasons. But usually other citizens may also apply and receive appointments—especially in areas where a particular party, which by law must be represented, does not have a good organization.

After they are appointed, it is normal for these persons to attend a short (one afternoon or evening) course of instruction in order to know what to do and not to do.

Watchers and challengers are the legal representatives of the political parties and other interested civic organizations, whose function can be inferred from their job titles. Their business is to check on each other, on individual voters, on fraud, and on illegal activities on the part of judges and other election officials and outsiders. They are especially concerned with challenging the right of individuals to vote and they frequently serve a very useful purpose by uncovering individuals who have no legal right to cast their ballots in a given precinct or at a certain polling place.

Other party workers are occasionally allowed to come into the polling place for consultation, to take messages, and the like. The policemen or detectives are there to receive and act on complaints or handle disturbances.

All states have fairly explicit laws on how polling places are to be set up, on procedures to be followed in setting up ballot boxes, arranging voting booths, handling the ballots, and processing the voters.

Other laws will prescribe the time for opening the polls, the duties of the officials, the nature and placement of the ballot box, the proportion of voting booths or machines to the number of voters, the number of voters who may be in the polling place at one time, and a long list of other requirements.

In most states the law also prescribes the time and manner of closing the polls and the counting (usually referred to as "tallying" or "canvassing") and reporting procedures. The same officials who administer the voting normally do the counting also. There are fairly stiff penalties for failure to conform to the legal regulations.

The counting of voting machine ballots is much simpler than counting paper ballots, the complete count for an entire city frequently being available within an hour or two after the closing of the polls. There are, however, strict rules on the use of voting machines, and they must be opened, repaired, sealed, and read according to precisely prescribed regulations.

Once the counting is done, the certified tally or canvass sheets are sent in to the central election board, which may, in turn, compile those counts which should be forwarded to the officials compiling, for example, the vote for a United States Senator. The secretary of state of an individual state is the person normally in charge of the entire state election administration process. He or other legally designated officials then certify to the United States Congress such voting tabulations as are required to decide elections to the federal offices.

Recounts may be demanded at certain points in this process. These may be authorized by the individuals or boards in charge of citywide, countywide, or statewide election administration. There are varying rules as to who shall bear the cost of the recount. Sometimes it is the government and other times it is the individual. If you are interested in a recount you had better see a lawyer—and quick!

The most crucial thing in election administration is to *know the law*. Your ignorance (if you are an official) may cost your party an election and, if it is mistaken for intent to defraud, may get you into serious trouble.

So, if you are going to serve on an election board or as a polling judge, inspector, or clerk, you will do well to listen quite carefully to any instruction available. If you are only a watcher or challenger, ignorance will not get you into much trouble unless you try to object to something that is perfectly legal. But if you do not know when somebody else is disobeying the law, you are not much use at your job.

3. POLICING THE ELECTION

All the above leads us to the problem of *election frauds*. The activities necessary to handle such matters have been described by the Republican National Committee as the "protective phase" of political work.

Let us consider this problem from the standpoint of (1) election officials, (2) political parties, and (3) other civic groups interested simply in honest elections.

Among the responsibilities of election officials is the prevention of fraud. This means, as has been emphasized before, that election officials need to be trained. They particularly need training in how to interpret the various laws regulating voting behavior and voting procedure. This is done in many places, but not as often nor as well as might be desired.

Therefore, if you have had only a minimum of instruction, and are planning to be an election official, you would do well to do a little more looking up on your own. Sometimes the secretary of state of individual states puts out special pamphlets. In Philadelphia the civic organization known as the Committee of Seventy also puts out a special folder entitled *Information for Voters—Watchers and Election Officers*, compiled from the Pennsylvania Election Code.

It is a good idea for any election official to have with him a copy of the state election code. At least check and find out where you can get more information in a hurry—in case you find you need it on election day. Then you will be prepared to cope with an emergency in a fairly intelligent way. And, if police are supposed to be assigned to your polling place, check and see if they are on the job.

From the standpoint of the political parties, the "protective phase" is also of great importance. There is no point in going to a lot of trouble only to be counted out. Nor do you want a lot of opposition party "ringers" or "floaters" voting who ought to have been challenged about their right to vote. Therefore, most political organizations spend a good deal of time in preparing party workers to be what are known as "challengers" or "checkers" or "poll watchers."

In its *Republican Workers' Manual*, the Republican National Committee recommends a training school for such workers as a must. The committee further suggests that a special "poll-watchers' manual" be prepared and used as the basis of this instruction. Normally each political party (and often other interested organizations) is entitled to have its own watchers and challengers at the polls. But they are of no use unless they are properly trained to do their job.

Prepare your poll-watching manual, select your personnel for the jobs, put them through a training school, and then back them up with action when the time comes. The work of the poll watchers should be especially coordinated with that of the law committee, mentioned before. For if anything is to be done, it usually must be done quickly and by experts who know their legal business.

Normally the activities of the political parties—engaged in checking on each other—will be sufficient to guarantee a fair and honest election. However, there sometimes is collusion between party workers in local areas. And, in some areas, there may be only one party with any real organization.

As a result, in some places—notably Chicago and New York—civic organizations of various kinds have undertaken quite extensive work on election day. In many places the Leagues of Women Voters sponsor poll-watching schools. Chambers of Commerce may set up special programs for the training of watchers. The same is often true of labor unions.

But the Joint Civic Committee on Elections in Chicago and the Honest Ballot Association in New York have gone the farthest in systematizing their work over the years. Both organizations recruit poll watchers from all kinds of sources: ministers, schoolteachers, students, civic-minded businessmen, and the like. They train them in a short course and then place them in all parts of the city. These persons are not just there unofficially but have the proper credentials entitling them to be watchers just the same as those representing any of the official political parties.

Here it is not possible to go into all the details of their arrangements, pamphlets, training schools, and the like. Write them directly if you wish more information. Much of their material applies only to the two cities in question, but it is appropriate to reproduce here some excerpts on *election frauds*. These should give you a good general idea of the problems involved and some of the things to look out for.

First, here is a section from the Joint Civic Committee's pamphlet entitled *Chicago's Fight for Honest Elections— Instructions to Observers*. Unfortunately this pamphlet is now out of print.

The Observation and Detection of Fraud

What is there for the observer to observe? It is true that, with one or two exceptions, our election laws are about as well-framed to eliminate voting frauds as is reasonably possible. The trouble does not lie with the law; the trouble comes from disregard of the law. The human element cannot be made angelic just by statute. Vote frauds are committed by human beings. Dishonest elections require dishonest judges and clerks and dishonest precinct captains and party workers. Vote frauds can best be prevented by the selection of careful and honest judges and clerks and by the punishment of those who turn out to be dishonest. Most of the judges and clerks who have served in the past and who will serve at the forthcoming elections are conscientious and upright men and women, but a sizable minority of them have not been, as is evident from the frequent parade of names in the contempt cases heard by the county court.

THE SUBSTITUTE JUDGE OR CLERK

It is quite possible that, in order to secure the presence on the precinct election board of officials who are dishonest, a regularly qualified judge or clerk of election may be "induced" to absent himself on election day. The "emergency" appointment of the "right" person may then be filled at 6:15 A.M. Even if the substitute is not in conspiracy with this movement, he is apt to be quite inexperienced and fraudulent practices may abound without his knowledge.

Observers should remember to note every sustained absence of a precinct election official and to identify each substitute official by name, address, and party affiliation.

If the officially appointed judge or clerk appears after a substitute has been appointed, he is required to take up his duties and the substitute is dismissed.

FRAUDULENT USE
OF APPLICATIONS FOR BALLOTS

The packages of official ballots and of applications for ballots, as well as the precinct binder and after election supplies and materials, are delivered to some one of the judges of election the day before election. These supplies are checked over by the judges of election to make sure that everything is in proper order for use the next day. Only on the morning of the election are the sealed packages and the sealed precinct binder to be opened. This must be done in full view of all those present, and only one package of each at a time should be opened. The rest of the packages remain sealed until needed.

The voter must sign the application for ballot in the polling place. This signature must be compared by two judges to ascertain that the person signing the application is the same person who signed the registration card. The registration card should be checked in the lower right-hand corner to see if that person has already voted on this election day.

But in certain precincts, judges of election sometimes permit a precinct captain or other party worker to take applications for ballots the night before election. Armed with these applications, the criminal attempts to induce the voter to sign the application in his home (in which event the ballot can be later marked as the criminal desires) or attempts himself to forge the voter's name. (In such cases, the signatures on the registration cards in the precinct binder are used as models.) Then the criminal, by use of these applications, secures a corresponding number of ballots and fraudulently votes them as he sees fit. This type of fraud cannot be committed without the connivance of the judges and clerks of election.

Forged applications are prepared outside the polling place and afterward brought in by the fraudulent voter. Careful observance will detect such a voter's failure to sign an application before the clerk in charge of applications and the production of a forged application from a pocket or handbag.

An attempt may be made toward the close of the day to put forged applications on the poll binder in order to bring the number of applications up to match any extra ballots which have illegally found their way into the ballot box.

To check this fraud, the observer should:

1. Be sure that the precinct binder is sealed on the morning of election day.

2. Be sure that all packages of official ballots and of applications for ballots are sealed on the morning of election day.

3. Be sure that only one package of official ballots is opened at one time.

4. Be sure that the judge in charge of the ballots counts the number of official ballots in each package as it is opened. There should be 100 in each package. Note any variations on your observer's report and request an explanation. Report by telephone what appears to you to be an illegal diversion of ballots.

5. Make an effort to see that two judges compare the signature on each application with the signature of that voter on his registration card. A practical approach to this problem is for the observer at irregular intervals to request a careful comparison in his presence as a spot check.

OMITTING TO INITIAL BALLOTS

By simple process on the part of the judge who is in charge of the ballots of omitting to initial the ballot given to any voter, the ballot becomes void and cannot be counted. A dishonest judge, who knows and opposes the political views of any voter, can disfranchise him by this means.

To prevent this fraud, the observer should watch every ballot as it is deposited in the ballot box to note the presence or absence of initials.

CHAIN VOTING

This type of vote fraud is common and hard to detect. The chain is started by obtaining a blank official ballot, either by stealing it, by getting it from a dishonest judge, by application for an absent voter's ballot made by a party worker who thus secures a ballot, or by a voter in the employ of the operator of the chain failing to deposit the ballot but instead delivering it to the operator of the chain. Sometimes the voter brings in a blank piece of paper that looks like a ballot, puts the ballot in his pocket, and slips the piece of paper in the ballot box when the judge's attention is diverted. The ballot is marked outside the polling place by the operator of the chain and is then given to a controlled worker who conceals it in his pocket and presents himself at the polls to cast his vote. This voter receives a ballot from the judge, goes to the voting booth, folds his new ballot and puts it in his pocket, takes out the ballot previously marked, leaves the voting booth, deposits the marked ballot with the judge at the ballot box, and outside the polls gives the unmarked ballot to the operator of the chain who then marks it as desired and starts the process over again. When the chain ends an attempt may be made to deposit the extra ballot or ballots in the ballot box.

The value of this fraud to the operator of the chain is that he knows that the votes are being cast "the right way." At about $.50 a head, a desired election result in some of the problem precincts can be obtained very easily and very cheaply. And the precinct captain, whose sole qualification for his political job is his ability to command the votes as desired in his precinct, has again proved his "fitness" for his position as an assistant to the organization.

This fraud can however be stopped, though it requires constant vigilance on the part of the observer who should:

1. Be sure that all packages of ballots are sealed on the morning of election day.

2. Be sure that only one package of ballots is opened at a time.

3. Be sure that each package of ballots contains exactly 100 ballots, and that the judge in charge counts these. Make a note of any variation and request an explanation.

4. Be sure that no ballot is initialed in advance.

5. Be sure that the judge hands out only one ballot at a time.

6. Be sure that every voter leaving the voting booth hands his ballot to the ballot judge, that he does not

personally deposit his ballot in the box and does not walk out with it.

7. Be sure that every ballot given to the judge after voting has on it the judge's initials. An absent voter's ballot used would not have such initials and could not be substituted for an initialed ballot. It could, however, be deposited when the judge was not looking and the initialed ballot carried out of the polling place to start a chain.

8. At irregular intervals during the day suggest a change in the judge who is initialing ballots thus causing a rotation of the judges doing this work. If the changes occur at irregular intervals previously initialed ballots may be discovered and the chain broken up.

9. Call committee ward headquarters and report suspected chain voting.

MISUSE OF THE ASSISTED VOTE

This method of vote fraud consists of compelling a voter to ask for assistance in marking his ballot, whether the voter needs assistance or not. If the voter does not conform to the request of the precinct captain in asking for assistance, he is not paid for his vote as agreed or is refused favors or reported as unqualified for patronage.

Once the voter has been intimidated by this means to ask for assistance, such will be given him by two precinct election officials (supposedly of opposite political parties but actually working with one political party) who will mark the ballot according to their wish and not according to the voter's wish. Too often only one election official will give the assistance or a precinct captain or other political worker is permitted to do so. All this, of course, is a flagrant violation of the letter and spirit of our election laws. Even precinct captains push voters around and walk into booths to "assist" them.

To prevent this fraud the observer should:

1. Be sure that no person receives assistance who does not qualify for it by reason of inability to read the English language, physical disability, or blindness.

2. Be sure that every voter who requests assistance (except for reason of apparent blindness) signs an affidavit that assistance is necessary.

3. Be sure that the assistance is given such voter only by two precinct election officials of opposite political parties.

4. Be sure that before the application for assistance is granted, the voter is thoroughly questioned. Particularly should this be the case where the voter has signed his registration card in English and nevertheless pleads inability to read the English language, as his reason for requesting assistance. (Note: Judges of election are required thoroughly to question the voter asking for assistance, checking all his answers with the information contained on the reverse side of the registration card.)

5. Be sure that the officials who render assistance sign the affidavit of the assisted voter that such assistance was given as the voter directed.

SOLICITATION OF VOTES

The law forbids electioneering or soliciting of votes within the polling place or within 100 feet of its entrance. The judges of election are charged with the responsibility of preventing such practice. Violation of this law may intimidate voters, preventing them from voting as they wish, even discouraging them from voting at all.

Observers should immediately report such violations.

REPEATERS

The same person may attempt to vote more than once during the day in the same precinct. A "repeater" may present a forged application under the name of a registered voter whom he knows will not present himself at the polls. He may also attempt to vote twice under the same name where he knows there are two cards in the precinct binder under the same name or under two like names distinguished only by an initial.

If the observer has a list of persons whose names appear on the precinct register although they are known to have moved from the precinct or to have died he should watch for "repeaters" attempting to vote under the names of such persons. The fact that ward and precinct workers have been trying to round up the soldier and sailor absentee vote may lead to organized attempts to vote under their names particularly if the worker has secured a specimen of the handwriting and knows the data on the registration record card. Watch this carefully. Detection of forged applications or affidavits will also aid the observer in preventing such attempts at illegal voting.

STUFFING THE BALLOT BOX

One method, not so widely used now because of the Permanent Registration Law in Illinois, consists of stuffing the ballot box. This procedure is just exactly what the name implies: the illegal deposit in the ballot box of official ballots marked by the criminal. If done in sufficient number, the election "result" may be swayed. Prior to the enactment of the Permanent Registration Law, this method was very effective. The only danger rested in detection at the time of stuffing. Now, however, ballots must be counted and made to agree in number with the applications for ballots on file in the poll binder. Excess ballots are destroyed. Stuffing the ballot box, to be effective, now requires a similar stuffing of the poll binder with applications for ballots. The requirement of agreement in number of ballots and applications has crimped this fraud, though not entirely stopped it.

To check this fraud the observer should:

1. Be at the polling place not later than 5:45 A.M.

2. See that the ballot box is empty when the polls open at 6 A.M. It must be shown to you.

3. See that each package of ballots is counted when opened. Note any variation from 100 and request an explanation. Report by phone what appears to you to be an illegal diversion of ballots.

4. See that the judges compare the number of voted ballots with the number of applications for ballots. They must agree in number; if not, the excess ballots must be destroyed.

5. Keep your own count of the ballots cast. This may easily be done by checking off the names on the printed precinct register, and the supplemental list, as persons vote.

6. See that the judge in charge of ballots initials only one at a time as called for.

7. See that the ballot box is kept in unobstructed view at all times. Incidents have been known where the precinct captain deliberately screened the ballot box with challengers and watchers of his own party to keep it from public view. Of course, this was done with the cooperation of a judge or judges of election.

8. See that an official at the count does not slop ballots onto the floor where planted ones could be picked up with them.

SHORT-PENCILING

This method of fraud is employed by dishonest judges after the polls have closed. A judge may cancel a vote by the simple process of marking the ballot in opposition to the voter's mark.

Short-penciling can be done when the judge handles the ballots after the close of the polls. Ingenuity on the part of the dishonest judge is the order of the day: he may conceal a short pencil in his hand as he sorts the ballots or he may use a bit of graphite on the fingernail, a bit of lead pencil fastened under the fingernail with sealing wax, a piece of lead pencil in a cigar or cigarette or fastened in a pencil eraser.

A variation of the short-penciling game is employed whenever the judge not only wishes to negate the vote cast for the opposing political party but wishes further to create a vote for his own. In such instances not only is the ballot short-penciled but the legitimate cross is erased.

To prevent this fraud the observer should be particularly watchful when the judges handle the ballots after the closing of the polls. The ballots should be kept completely on the table in full view and no one should touch them except the judges.

FRAUDULENT COUNTING AND TALLYING
OF VOTES AND MAKING RETURNS

During the count of the ballots dishonest judges may call the votes improperly as they read them to the clerks who tally these votes. Similarly, the judges may call the votes properly but the clerks may tally them for other candidates.

Fraud can be committed in the transfer of the vote total from the tally sheets onto the statement of votes. These vote totals should be compared and the observer should see that every one of the judges and clerks signs the statement of votes.

After all this is done the observer should accompany the judges and clerks to the office of the Board of Election Commissioners to make sure that no change is made before the election materials are handed in.

CONCLUSION

Fraudulent election practices flourish under cover. Dishonesties such as are related above certainly will be deterred by the presence in the polls of trained observers who will stay on the job until the election is completed.

The procedural essentials for poll-watching in New York City have been outlined by the Honest Ballot Association on the last page of an *Instructions for Watchers* pamphlet. The bulk of this list would apply anywhere.

Fifteen Points

1. Be at the polling place not later than 5:30 A.M.

2. Locate nearest telephone to the polling place before entering. Be provided with at least six nickels for phone calls, this book, and a pencil.

3. Exhibit your watcher's certificate promptly to the chairman of the Board of Inspectors and to the police officer.

4. Enter as soon as possible on the tally sheet furnished you the names and addresses of:

    a. all four inspectors of election, the clerks, and their respective parties;

    b. captains for all parties;

    c. shield numbers of the two police officers assigned to your polling place (inside and outside),

and mail tally sheet as soon as possible after close of election.

5. Do not leave the polling place under any circumstances unless you are relieved. For relief, call your local headquarters or the HBA.

6. See that all counters on the voting machine read zero at the opening of the polls. Otherwise make necessary record.

7. Watch voting machine. Do not permit tampering, defacing, switching of names, spying through holes in curtains, or other illegal practices.

8. See that all unauthorized persons are kept outside of the guard rail at all times. One watcher from each party or independent body may be inside the guard rail at all times. During the count, two watchers.

9. Do not permit electioneering within, or within 100 feet of, the polling place.

10. If the voter is recorded in the registration book as entitled to assistance, then, and then only, may he at his request have assistance of two inspectors of different political faiths, or, if the specified physical disability is manifest, assistance of his father, mother, brother, sister, wife, or child instead.

11. If you make an arrest for a violation of the election law, telephone your own headquarters or the HBA to send relief at once.

12. Do not forget that you have the right to challenge any voter who is a suspect or who is not entitled to vote in the district. Also that it is the *duty* of the Inspectors to challenge *everyone* on the "challenge list."

13. Should the machine get out of order, telephone the Board of Elections . . . and also the HBA at once.

14. All persons *in line* at the hour set for the closing of the polls are entitled to vote.

15. When the count is being recorded one HBA watcher should carefully check each counter in back of

the machine as the figures are called off, while another HBA watcher verifies the proper recording of the vote in the statement of canvass and the return.

In general, be polite but firm. Do not allow yourself to be browbeaten by anyone. You have rights, established by law. Assert them courteously.

Whenever necessary bring to the police officer's attention the duties imposed on him by law and by his department's rules and regulations.

4. EVALUATION

When the election is over, there are a few matters—win or lose—that must be taken care of immediately. The current *County GOP Leader's Manual* of the Republican National Committee, almost the only such manual which outlines a year-round political organization plan, notes the most important (see Figure 9 on the next page.)

As both Republicans and Democrats agree, the next step is *evaluation*. This is a research step and much in Chapter 8 is relevant at this point. But a broadside put out by the Democratic National Committee in anticipation of the 1960 election sums up the process well.

Where Do We Go From Here?

Elections are won *between* campaigns. Elections are won in the precincts. Elections are won because a *permanent* political organization is prepared to win. These are the truisms of politics.

Victory is wonderful but it will last only two years unless we figure out how to capitalize on that victory. Below is an *evaluation program* that is the first step toward victory in 1960.

SEND OUT AN EVALUATION QUESTIONNAIRE

Use your campaign volunteer list, your active party membership list, and your roster of candidates to mail out an evaluation questionnaire (it can be a mimeo-

PAGE 1. **NOV EVEN YEAR**

PAY ALL BILLS promptly

SOOTHE any ruffled feelings that were developed in the "nervous" days of the campaign

BE GENEROUS with "THANK YOU'S" by letter by telephone and in person to:

DONORS of money

DEFEATED candidates

WINNING candidates

HOLDOVER officeholders (Even if they didn't do much, you may embarrass them into helping more next time.)

COMMITTEEMEN

COMMITTEEWOMEN

PRECINCT workers

VOLUNTEERS for candidates

POTENTIAL donors and workers

WHOEVER else helped in the election last month

ESTABLISH rapport and liaison with your winners to get their administrations off the ground successfully

BE SEEN in your Courthouse

Figure 9

graphed self-mailer if funds are low). Here are some suggested questions:

1. *What, in your opinion, were the strong points of the campaign?* Mention techniques used by individual candidates; special programs; activities; literature; newspaper, radio and TV publicity; popular gimmicks.

2. *What, in your opinion, were the weak points of the campaign?* Did we fail to develop good ideas? Did we start too late on certain activities? Did we underestimate the effect of certain issues? Did we lack sufficient information on election laws or procedures? Should we begin work to change some laws? Did we have too few workers or too few well-trained workers?

3. *What ideas for future improvement did you get from your observation or experience in this campaign?*

4. *How, in your opinion, can we build a stronger Democratic Party organization?*

ANALYZE THE ELECTION RETURNS

Get a complete set of the election returns for your area. Compare them with previous elections to spot areas where the Democratic Party is losing strength. Compare the returns with the precinct organization to spot any area where the organization is weak.

HOLD A SERIES OF EVALUATION MEETINGS

Start at the town and county level. Invite all who participated in the campaign to be represented: party officials, candidates' campaign workers, women's groups, Young Democrats, Teen Dems, representatives of special campaign committees, volunteers of all kinds (particularly some of the new people who worked for the first time to get some fresh viewpoints). Follow up with a representative statewide meeting. If a statewide meeting cannot be called, arrange for a special panel discussion at the next large Democratic gathering in the state. By all means send a report on the local evaluation session to the state headquarters.

BEGIN BUILDING A VICTORY FILE

Collect samples of effective campaign literature, good newspaper ads, good radio or TV scripts, samples of popular give-away items (and where they can be purchased). *Make sure that you keep all mailing lists and all lists of volunteer workers.* Ask the people who headed up special campaign projects to write reports on the activities of their groups and include in them samples of special appeal letters, programs, information on costs and procedures.

MAKE A POINT OF KEEPING THE NEW PEOPLE WHO HELPED IN THIS CAMPAIGN ACTIVE UNTIL THE NEXT ONE

Get lists from candidates of their good workers and make sure they are invited to all victory celebrations. Be sure the precinct captains and workers in their area know of their interest and activity. Invite these newcomers to join clubs or help them organize new ones in areas where none exist.

5. CONCLUSION

However your evaluation turns out, you can be sure of one thing—within a few days the entire process outlined in this book must commence all over again. Therefore it is appropriate to conclude both this chapter and the book with a short excerpt from the Democratic National Committee's *County Handbook,* designed to prepare you for the next cycle of political action.

Between Campaigns

Elections are won between campaigns. Following is a checklist of activities, based on successful practices:

1. Regular meetings help to keep up the cooperative spirit.

2. Public recognition of workers who have done good jobs keeps them active.

3. Discussion of issues in small and large meetings maintains interest.

4. Committees operate the year around:

    a. The registration chairman watches out for

newly naturalized citizens; keeps lists of high school graduates and sends them reminders to register as they come of age; keeps his records current as people move in and out of the county. Work to liberalize registration laws is most important between campaigns.

b. The Finance Chairman continues to solicit pledges and contributions, sell *Democratic Digests,* and promote fund-raising projects.

c. The speakers chairman trains speakers and promotes engagements for them.

d. The publicity chairman publicizes all events as usual.

e. The research chairman keeps files current to avoid a last minute rush when campaign time comes around again.

f. Precinct leaders and workers keep their records on the voters up to date; watch out for the welfare of the precinct; visit newcomers; help with public problems such as street repairs, recreational facilities; participate in service organizations and in community activities, such as fund drives, celebrations of patriotic holidays, and other civic projects.

Chapter 14

Where
to Go
for More

The purpose of this chapter is to give you some further idea of the sources from which this book has been developed, and to offer suggestions about where to go for more information.

No attempt has been made to relist here all the items which have been mentioned in Chapters 1 through 13. Therefore, if you wish to look for references on a subject, such as "election administration," proceed as follows: (1) check the index, (2) look under the "election administration" heading in Chapter 13, and (3) then at the supplementary listing for Chapter 13 contained here. That is, the references below are organized to match the subject matter of the preceding chapters.

CHAPTER 1

For a good, short treatment of the American party system, see *The Role of Political Parties U.S.A.*, prepared by Joseph C. Harsch and Frederick W. Collins in 1962 for the League of Women Voters Education Fund (1026 Seventeenth St., N.W., Washington 6, D.C.). *Politics in the American States*, edited by Herbert Jacob and Kenneth N. Vines (Boston, 1965), is a most useful comparative analysis. Exceedingly comprehensive and a major college text on all aspects of politics and political behavior is *Politics, Parties, and Pressure Groups*, 5th ed., by V. O. Key, Jr. (New York, 1964). For a shorter, paperback version, see Howard Penniman, *The American Political Process* (New York, 1962). Both major parties have pamphlet histories available from their national headquarters, but for the single most complete volume see Wilfred E. Binkley, *American Political Parties: Their Natural History*, 3rd ed. (New York, 1959). For an excellent series of short, popular publications on many aspects of American politics—beginning with *Who, Me a Politician* by Donald G. Herzberg, Director of the Eagleton Institute of Politics at Rutgers—write the Center for Information on America, Washington, Connecticut.

CHAPTER 2

For the most complete analyses of independence and nonpartisanship among voters see Robert E. Lane, *Political Life* (New York, 1959), pp. 175–80; Angus Campbell *et al.*, *The American Voter* (New York, 1960); and Eugene C. Lee, *The Politics of Nonpartisanship* (Berkeley, Calif., 1960).

CHAPTER 3

The most lively and exciting compilation on the subject of this chapter is *The Political Vocation*, a series of sixty-five selections edited by Paul Tillett (New York, 1965). Some especially relevant works by practicing politicians, besides those quoted in this chapter or elsewhere in the book, include Edward J. Flynn (former Democratic National Chairman), *You're the Boss* (New York, 1947); Raymond E. Baldwin (former governor and congressman of Connecticut), *Let's Go Into Politics* (New York, 1952); Fuller Warren (former governor of Florida), *How to Win in Politics* (Tallahassee, Fla., 1949); and Robert H. Miller (treasurer, Chautauqua County, N.Y.), *Politics Is People* (New York, 1962). *Politics U.S.A.*, edited by James M. Cannon (New York, 1960), is a symposium on political action, each chapter written by someone knowledgeable concerning political life and practices, varying from Mrs. Charles A. Halleck, "On Being a Politician's Wife," to Richard M. Nixon, "The Importance of Homework" and Sig Michelson, President of CBS News, "The Use of Television." Besides being autobiographical, all these books contain practical advice on the tactics and techniques of political action.

CHAPTER 4

Oddly enough, there is relatively little published on "how to get into politics." Much of what is available appears in this chapter. However, write the young voter organizations of both the Republicans and the Democrats—addressing the Young Republican National Leadership Training Institute, Inc., or the Young Democratic Clubs of America in care of their respective national headquarters. See also Part I, "Becoming a Politician," of Marshall Loeb and William Safire, *Plunging Into Politics* (New York, 1964); Paul Douglass and Alice McMahon, *How to Be an Active Citizen* (Gainesville, Fla., 1960); and chap. 1, "How to Get Started" in the current edition of *How to Win* (AFL-CIO Committee on Political Education).

Materials on parliamentary procedure and the conduct of meetings are more readily available. The best single source is, of course, *Robert's Rules of Order*. This may be purchased almost anywhere. Other compilations will do and there are a good many useful summaries for quick reference purposes. One of the best manuals to use for training groups in parliamentary procedure is O. Garfield Jones' *Senior Manual for Group Leadership* (New York: Appleton-Century-Crofts). Another excellent guide is the *Standard Code of Parliamentary Procedure* by Alice F. Sturgis (New York: McGraw Hill). For a first-rate general guide to the conduct of meetings, including a section on "how to draft constitution and bylaws," see *Successful Leadership in Groups and Organizations* by Joseph A. Wagner (San Francisco: Chandler Publishing Company).

Town meetings present special problems. Here see *Connecticut Town Meeting* (Institute of Public Service, University of Connecticut), or *A Handbook for Town Moderators*, by Geoffrey Bolton (Massachusetts Federation of Taxpayers Associations, Inc., 11 Beacon St., Boston).

CHAPTER 5

There is really no good comprehensive work on local political organization, and the best there are have gone out of print. If you can get hold of them, by all means see the Republican National Committee's 88-page *Campaign Manual*, published in the 1950s; and the *Manual of Practical Political Action*, edited by L. C. Frank, Jr. and R. E. Shikes and put out in the late 1940s by the National Citizens Political Action Committee, then an arm of the Progressive Party operating out of New York City. A number of the works already cited also contains sections on political organization; see, for example, chap. 13, "Building the Organization" in Marshall Loeb and William Safire, *Plunging Into Politics* (New York, 1964).

CHAPTER 6

Again, there are no comprehensive items on the subject. Write the agencies mentioned in the text.

CHAPTER 7

Other than those already cited in this chapter, the principal studies on campaign finances are those of the Citizen's Research Foundation (245 Nassau St., Princeton, N.J.). See especially, *Financing the 1960 Election* (1962) and *Responsibility in Party Finance* (1963), both by Herbert E. Alexander.

For techniques in Illinois, see James C. Worth, "Political Fund Raising Today" in *Politics, U.S.A.* (New York, 1960), edited by James A. Cannon. Also, see Maurice McCaffrey, "Budgets" in *Advertising Wins Elections* (Minneapolis, 1962); Alexander Heard, "A New Approach to Campaign Finances," *The New York Times Magazine* (Oct. 6, 1963); and *Financing Presidential Campaigns*, a report of the President's Commission on Campaign Costs (Washington, D.C., 1962). The problem of financing the 1964 campaign is most fully treated in "The Switch in Campaign Giving" by Herbert E. Alexander and Harold B. Meyers in *Fortune* (November, 1965).

CHAPTER 8

For what is known about American voting behavior, see Robert E. Lane, *Political Life* (New York, 1959); Angus Campbell *et al., The American Voter* (New York, 1960); Hugh A. Bone and Austin Ranney, *Politics and Voters* (New York, 1963); Lester W. Milbrath, *Political Participation* (Chicago, 1965); Richard M. Scammon, "Why One Third of Us Don't Vote," *The New York Times Magazine* (Nov. 17, 1963); and the *Report* of the President's Commission on Registration and Voting (Washington, D.C., 1963).

For assistance in the social analysis of a voting district a useful item for the ordinary citizen is *The Study of Local Politics* by William H. Riker (New York, 1959). In undertaking position and issue research, see *Local Political Surveys* by E. E. Schattschneider and Victor Jones (New York, 1962).

Polling is for the professional, but an amateur can gain

considerable insight from *How to Take a Survey of Public Opinion*, an eight-page pamphlet for the beginner by R. W. Burckhardt and M. O. Sawyer (National Council for the Social Studies, Washington, D.C.); and Riker's *The Study of Local Politics*, cited above. If you have mastered these, then go to *Social Research* by Charles H. Backstrom and Gerald D. Hursh (Evanston, Ill., 1963), designed to be a "handbook for research in political behavior." On the growing rapprochement between the political and academic worlds, especially relevant here, see Robert C. Wood, "A 'Brain Trust' for Every Smoke-Flled Room," *The New York Times Magazine* (May 15, 1960).

CHAPTER 9

The relevant literature on campaigning is enormous. Again, biography and history are important sources. For some more pinpointed discussions, see Robert E. Merriam and Rachel M. Goetz, *Going Into Politics* (New York, 1957), chap. 7; Stimson Bullitt, *To Be a Politician* (New York, 1959), chap. 5; James Ertel, *How to Run for Office* (New York, 1960), chap. 5; James A. Cannon, ed., *Politics U.S.A.* (New York, 1960), Part III; and Marshall Loeb and William Safire, *Plunging Into Politics* (New York, 1964), Part II.

For an even more extensive "timetable," covering a two-year span, see the 1964 *County GOP Leader's Manual*, published by the Republican National Committee.

CHAPTER 10

Many of the items already cited are useful "on being a candidate," but see especially those listed under Chapters 3 and 9. In addition, see Chaps. 5 and 9 of *How to Go Into Politics* by Hugh D. Scott, Jr. (New York, 1949) and the 1964 *Democratic Campaign Manual* of the Democratic National Committe.

CHAPTER 11

The literature on publicity and public relations is vast. However, for political purposes two items stand out: *Professional Public Relations and Political Power* by Stanley Kelley, Jr. (Baltimore, 1956); and *Advertising Wins Elections* by Maurice McCaffrey (Minneapolis, 1962).

CHAPTER 12

The principal item here, other than sources cited in the text, is *How to Win Votes and Influence Elections* by Don Pirie Cass (Chicago, 1962). This is a general guide to precinct work and canvassing, based in large part on interviews with a number of practicing precinct commitemen.

CHAPTER 13

There is no general work on election day activities alone. For more information than is given here one must go to a volume on political parties, such as that by V. O. Key, Jr., cited above under the references for Chapter 1.

Index